World Peace and the Human Family

Television news is dominated by images of violence and warfare. The media suggest that war is a ubiquitous feature of contemporary society. History can convince us that it has ever been so, and many theorists of international relations argue that nothing is likely to change. Yet Roy Weatherford argues in this book that we are on the verge of a profound change in human relations – the end of the sovereignty of nation-states and the warfare between them, and the beginning of the rule of democratically established, collectively enforced international law. He proposes that national sovereignty and jingoistic provincialism must yield to a world culture, speaking a world language, subject to a world government and living as a worldwide family – the human family.

For too long world peace has seemed a noble but unattainable ideal. Weatherford shows that it is now both economically and politically possible – and is therefore our moral duty.

Roy Weatherford is Professor of Philosophy at the University of South Florida. His publications include *The Implications of Determinism* (1991).

POINTS OF CONFLICT

A new series from Routledge

The books in this series mark a new departure in academic publishing. Written by philosophers, or from a philosophical standpoint, their purpose is to probe beneath the shibboleths of day-to-day debate and controversy on important social and political topics. Common to all the authors is a view of the importance of the analytical skills of the professional thinker in reaching decisions on the large issues of our time. The books challenge the assumptions that lie behind the headlines and offer proposals, not always the expected ones, for action.

Also available:

Aids and the Good Society
Patricia Illingworth

Understanding War
W. B. Gallie

Terrorism and Collective Responsibility
Burleigh Taylor Wilkins

World Peace and the Human Family

Roy Weatherford

ROUTLEDGE

London and New York

First published 1993
by Routledge
11 New Fetter Lane, London EC4P 4EE

Simultaneously published in the USA and Canada
by Routledge
29 West 35th Street, New York, NY 10001

Phototypeset by Intype, London
Printed in Great Britain by Clays Ltd, St Ives plc

British Library Cataloguing in Publication Data
Weatherford, Roy
World Peace and the Human Family. –
(Points of Conflict)
I. Title II. Series
327.1

Library of Congress Cataloging-in-Publication Data
Weatherford, Roy
World peace and the human family / Roy Weatherford.
p. cm.—(Points of conflict)
Includes bibliographical references and index.
1. Peace. 2. International organization. 3. Social ethics.
4. Social sciences—Philosophy. I. Title. II. Series.
JX1953.W39 1993
341.2—dc20 92-36242

ISBN 0-415-06302-7
ISBN 0-415-06303-5 (pb)

To my darling daughter
MARGARET MARIE 'MEG' WEATHERFORD
who gives me reason to wish for world peace,
and cause to hope that it is attainable.

Contents

Preface

This series is designed to bring the skills of the technically trained philosopher to bear upon the important and controversial issues of the day.

I have in fact been trained in the Anglo-American tradition of analytic philosophy. My PhD is from Harvard University, where my chief influences were Roderick Firth in Ethics and Epistemology; Israel Scheffler in Epistemology and Science; W.V.O. Quine in Logic, Language, and Epistemology; John Rawls in Ethics; and Hilary Putnam in everything.

My first two books were *Philosophical Foundations of Probability Theory* and *The Implications of Determinism*, both moderately technical works involving much explication and criticism of the views of other philosophers.

This book, on the other hand, is not technical philosophy in the usual sense, it is more like philosophy in the grand manner – it seeks to understand the world in important ways and dares to suggest how the world *should* be.

This is primarily a work in social philosophy and ethics. It deals with the nature of human culture, ideal political structures, our mutual duties, and the moral foundations of pluralism. It is rooted in empiricism and pragmatism, and takes it as given that all that we know we learn from experience and that there are no *a priori* truths or absolute values. It has been shaped by what I call the Harvard Paradigm: the metaphilosophical view that in all branches of knowledge we sometimes adjust our theories to fit the evidence, but we also sometimes adjust the evidence to fit our theories. There can in principle be no general rule to tell us which to adjust in any given situation. These decisions, as Quine says, are 'where rational, pragmatic.'

My thesis is that world peace is both desirable and achievable through a world government and a world culture rooted in the notion of the human family.

While this thesis is increasingly popular, there are still many intellectual and practical obstacles. Despite the spirit of the age, there remain a few who think world peace is not desirable. More importantly, there are many who think it is not achievable.

The same is true – or even more so – of the notion of the human family. A great many think that it is too idealistic or too socialistic. Some there are who think that families aren't that great anyway, and constitute a poor model for society at large.

No doubt the greatest objections are to my belief that there should be an effective world government, at the expense of national sovereignty, and a world language to supplement and eventually supplant the mutually unintelligible local languages of today.

My arguments are partly empirical generalizations, based on my observations of human beings and my interpretation of world events. They are also partly theoretical constructions based on my view of ethics and obligation.

The most controversial of my formal claims is that our moral obligations to others are ordered in direct relationship to the social distance obtaining between us. The most controversial of my empirical conclusions is my technological optimism and conviction that despite (and partly because of) the horrible stories we see in the news media every day, the world is in fact getting to be a better place and it is within our power to make it very pleasant indeed.

Because the book is didactic in nature, I have somewhat relaxed the strictures of scholarship that would be appropriate in a more technical work. I have not, for example, tried to include every article ever written on these topics or to document every paragraph that has shaped my thinking. Most of the references to other works I have tried to move into notes, where the scholar can find them but they will not intrude into the argumentation. Ideas and arguments that are common currency I have not bothered to pedigree – many of these concepts have been around for a long time and are readily accessible in general philosophical works.

My intention has been, throughout, to try to convince the intelligent and moderately well-educated reader of the desirability and attainability of a controversial but very important vision of how the world should be.

It is impossible to thank or even to remember the many people who have helped to shape my ideas on this enormous topic. Clearly my parents Opal Wynona Luter Weatherford and the late Reverend Frank Carter Weatherford set me on the path of trying to improve the world. My wife and intellectual colloquist of many years, Doris Weatherford, has taken many hours away from writing her own books to help straighten out parts of mine, and to help me understand the world in general and the importance of critical historical thinking from varied perspectives in particular. For the first time, as we worked on our respective third books, our subject matter intersected to the extent that I have actually excerpted a couple of paragraphs of her work, a mild form of nepotism for which I trust Prentice-Hall will forgive me.

My daughter, Margaret Marie 'Meg' Weatherford, to whom this book is dedicated, has gone away to Harvard to advance her own education, but she remains in my heart as an example of much that is good in the world and an incentive to continue working for a better future. Hilary Putnam has again been generous with his time and advice. Robert A. Schultz has shared his passion for world peace and provided me with literature from the organization 'Beyond War,' where I have found much that is congenial to my way of thinking, especially the central idea that 'War is obsolete.' My union, the National

Education Association, continues to be one of the great altruistic forces for world peace through education. And the University of South Florida and my colleagues in the Department of Philosophy continue to encourage me and even pay me for what I love to do.

1 World peace as an ideal

A casual student of history might well be excused for drawing the conclusion that war is *the* most characteristic feature of human society. Indeed, until the present century, much of what most people thought of as history and much that was taught in the schools as history was the recounting of wars and rebellions, conquests and reigns, battles and bullets. Our human energy found its most powerful expression in the massive forces we mobilized in order to kill or overcome each other. It is not a promising history from which to extrapolate world peace.

Depending on how one individuates wars, it is possible that there has not been a day for the last 5,000 years when some human beings were not at war with some others. (Don't forget, most such calculations concern themselves only with European nation-states and ignore the tribal warfare prevalent in the majority of the world in the past.)

But extrapolation is a tricky thing. Until the development of balloons, there had never been a day when it was not true that all human beings were on the surface of the earth. Within two centuries it became clear that there would never again be such a day. Until 1961, there had never been a day when human beings existed outside Earth's atmosphere. In three decades we may already have passed the last day when there were no human beings in space. Before the work of Jenner and others, there had been a dreary history of constant deaths from smallpox, with whole tribes being destroyed as the Europeans spread it around the world. At this moment, no human being suffers from smallpox, and, we may reasonably hope, none will ever again.

The scourges and limitations of human life are not eternal constants – many of them can be overcome by a combination of knowledge and wisdom. It is my belief that war, like slavery and cannibalism, is a temporary evil in human society, rather than a permanent condition. It can be abolished, and the best way to abolish it is by developing a global society in which the human family is governed by an effective world government.

It is frequently said that achieving world peace is the most important goal humanity should pursue. As it happens, I do not think this is so. I believe, to the contrary, that the most important goal we can pursue at the present time is the development of space travel.

I hold this somewhat unorthodox view because, though I share with the pacifists the view that preservation of the species is the *sine qua non* for all other possible goods, I believe that war is only one of many possible threats to human existence and not necessarily the most dangerous one.

Despite the horrors of war, we have not only managed to survive many bloody encounters, we have actually increased in numbers to the point where there are clearly too many of us in the world at present. (While I'm attacking liberal shibboleths, I might as well mention that I also reject the view that overpopulation is our greatest threat. I agree with the goals and most of the arguments of such groups as Zero Population Growth, but overpopulation is inherently and necessarily a self-limiting problem – when overpopulation reaches the point where billions of people starve, the population will either diminish or stabilize; it cannot go on until *everyone* dies of overpopulation!)

Furthermore, although nuclear weapons bring a new level of horror and destruction to warfare, we have survived their actual use and subsequent worldwide deployment until now. It is not even settled in my mind that we would *all* die in a general nuclear holocaust – it *is* settled in my mind that we would all die if the sun were to explode into a nova, as it certainly will some day. We might also see the end of human existence as the result of an asteroid collision (a frequently argued cause of the extinction of the dinosaurs), attack from extra-terrestrials, a universal and always fatal epidemic (perhaps AIDS is just a warm-up effort . . .), or some yet-to-be-encountered horror we cannot even imagine.

In any event, the current situation is such that we are totally dependent for our survival as a species on the continued existence of one planet in a benign state, with relatively narrow limitations on such things as temperature range, level of radioactivity, atmospheric composition, and so on. The most important single thing we can do as a species is to end that state of dependence by spreading ourselves throughout the solar system, the galaxy, and then the universe. Or, as we used to say in the Army, 'Let's have a little dispersion there – one round will kill you all!'

In addition to disagreeing with the pacifists about the priority of peace as a goal, I also disagree with the extreme pacifist claim that violence is always and everywhere immoral. No doubt it is repugnant, usually it is wrong, but sometimes it is the lesser of two evils and morally permissible. Even war itself might sometimes be justified, as Just War theorists have argued and as most people in fact believe about the Allies' participation in World War II. It does not follow that war is either desirable or generally excusable. War merely takes its place as one of a range of possible human activities that must be judged contextually and practically rather than proscribed absolutely.

Having said all that, I am now going to devote the rest of this book to an attempt to establish that world peace is in fact highly desirable and practically attainable. I am, if you will, a pragmatic pacifist.

Christianity

The conception that world peace is a religious ideal and moral duty is common to most religions.

Christianity, in particular, thinks of itself as a peaceful religion, and is fond of calling its founder 'The Prince of Peace.'

The notion that Peace should have a Prince suggests that it is not merely a negativity, the end of fighting, but something positive to be established, and this, too, is an idea that is frequently found throughout history.

It is commonly held that the early Christian church was avowedly pacifist and only changed its approach when corrupted by the Constantinian compromise.[1] Certainly the spectacles of armed bishops and military crusades against the infidels have embarrassed serious Christians for generations. But these aberrations, though illustrative of the enormous moral flexibility of religious leaders, are only viewed as embarrassments because they are held *not* to be in accordance with the fundamental tradition taught by Christ, the tradition of peace. (Christ's famous remark 'Do not think that I have come to bring peace on earth; I have not come to bring peace, but a sword'[2] is usually construed as an attempt to shatter domestic tranquility and complacency rather than to incite warfare, but, taken out of context, it certainly doesn't sound like a Prince of Peace, does it?)

Emily Balch has suggested a positive conception of Christian peace:

> Peace we must conceive not as an empty negation of conflict. We want life, the more abundant life that Christ came to bring, and life is a current of energy. Conflicting currents waste and confuse and often merely cancel one another. Current added to current gives added fullness, speed, depth, power. This is peace – the full flowing harmony of active wills.[3]

Other religions, similarly, have urged or mandated that their believers pursue the goal of universal peace. Even the secular religion of Marxism/Leninism professes peace as its goal.

Marxism/Leninism

In the *Communist Manifesto* Marx and Engels called on the 'working men [*sic*] of all countries' to unite.[4] In subsequent writings, and in his support of the Internationals, Marx made it clear that workers all over the world were comrades in the class struggle. Further, since the class struggle is the engine that drives both nationalism and warfare, the final victory of the proletariat over the bourgeoisie will usher in a period of world peace. Finally, when the conditions are at hand society as a whole will govern its economic life by the same principle we see at work in loving families: 'From each according to his ability, to each according to his needs!'[5]

Since the majority of people in the world – indeed, the majority of governments – profess to be devoted followers of a peaceful religion (or of Marxism), how does it happen that we are, nevertheless, constantly subjected to war?

Not taken seriously

One obvious possibility is that those who publicly espouse the noble goal of peace do so hypocritically, and do not really take it seriously.

Consider, for example, the existence of religious wars throughout the centuries. It is possible to raise a serious argument that the existence of religion has *caused* more warfare than it has prevented or ameliorated. Whether or not this extreme claim is true, clearly religions have not managed to bring about world peace and have, on the contrary, been all too eager to justify and sanctify whatever conflict the civil authority chooses to pursue.

Religions also have not succeeded in making people moral (though here there is more evidence that they have contributed significantly to that effort). One explanation may be that the historical refinement of the religious impulse having culminated in a perfect divinity, it seems inevitable that our religiously founded moral duty must also aim at perfection. Thus we have the phenomenon of people giving up on trying to be good (or driving themselves to neurotic despair) because they cannot attain the perfection they have been told is obligatory. F. H. Bradley is one of the few philosophers who has taken this problem seriously and offered a solution.[6] My own view, as developed in the penultimate chapter of this book, also addresses this issue, and lowers our moral sights to a more attainably human standard of conduct, but let us set this aside for now.

History of the idea of peace

The philosophical history of the idea of peace is also a long one. It includes many different conceptions of why peace is necessary and how it is to be brought about. As J. T. Johnson has put it:

> The quest for peace . . . is not a new creature of the nuclear age. It has a tradition; rather, the quest for peace has developed through several distinguishable moral traditions, each of which can be identified in the present historical context. . . . I identify three such moral traditions of the quest for peace. . . . The three are the just war tradition of setting limits to war, the sectarian pacifism of withdrawal from the world and its ills, and the political tradition of thought that finds the cure for discord among nations in the establishment of a new, more universal, and rightly constituted political order.[7]

Of Johnson's three traditions, I believe the first, the concept of a just war, has served a useful historical purpose in gradually civilizing our views about war. The second, the sectarian pacifisms of the Waldensians, the Jehovah's Witnesses and so on, have, on the whole, seemed fundamentally private views about personal moral obligations that never gained wide acceptance and, hence, have played a relatively small part in our story. (The Society of Friends may be treated as an exception here, since its modern tradition has leaned towards involvement with the world and an attempt to reform it.)

Clearly my views fall in the third of these traditions. The final achievement of world peace, I believe, will be encouraged and sustained by the moral support to be found in the first two traditions, but it will be made possible only through practical politics.

This third tradition, Johnson says,

> coalesces most visibly in the thought of Renaissance humanism, most specifically in the writings of Erasmus. Broadly speaking, it envisions the solution of the problem of war to be in the creation of a more inclusive society, a 'superstate,' in which (because there will no longer be petty states to squabble among themselves) there will be no wars. This is the core concept right along from Erasmus's medieval forebears through his own writings to the 'perpetual peace' theorists of the Enlightenment era to nineteenth- and twentieth-century internationalism.[8]

The 'superstate' may be either a universal state, as Dante preferred, or one or more individual states acting locally to eliminate war and bring internal and external peace to their vicinity, as Marsilius of Padua and Rousseau preferred.[9]

Among perpetual peace theorists, I give pride of place to Immanuel Kant.[10] I believe that he was right about the moral imperative for world peace, and he was almost right about the way to achieve it. When he set forth his proposal for perpetual peace he said, 'The postulate which is basic to all the following articles is: All men who can reciprocally influence each other must stand under some civil constitution.'[11]

Just so! We must escape the state of nature that obtains among nations, and to do so we must have a world government.

Conceptual rejection of peace

Not everyone, of course, has even professed to accept the goal of universal peace as desirable and obtainable.

The most widespread and powerful rejection of peace as desirable is the fascistic tendency of nationalism, leavened with a pseudo-Darwinian belief in the developmental desirability of conflict.

Fascism is fundamentally the attitude or idea that the state is the most basic, important, and admirable unit of existence. It sees all values as subordinate to the state, all individuals as having importance only as citizens of the state, and all actions to be judged primarily by how they do or do not contribute to the glory of the state. Since war has historically been the 'natural' source of glory for states, Fascism has a strong, perhaps inevitable, tendency to embrace war as an instrument of national policy.

In partial justification of this policy, modern Fascists tend to argue that the 'purification' of war will weed out those who are unsuitable for survival and thereby guarantee the ascendancy of the 'master race.' Thus war is justified as a biological, as well as a spiritual, imperative of the state.

The horrors of the Fascist states of World War II have done much to discredit this view, but it lurks there yet, in the heart of every jingoist who lusts for war, no doubt, but also in the soul of every 'ordinary citizen' who exults in victory and despises foreigners.

The principal argument that war is inevitable, however, does not require that war be viewed as a good – it merely states that human nature is such that we always have used and (therefore) always will use violence to settle our differences, protect our own existence, and achieve dominance over others. This behavior is seen to be as natural to us as head-butting is to mountain goats, and as little susceptible to revision.

Certainly there is a great deal in human history to motivate such pessimism. We have suffered through so much that is horrible – wars, rapes, despotism, cannibalism, sexism, racism, and slavery – that tough-minded individuals feel justified in dismissing pacifists as 'idealists' who are out of touch with reality and pursuing an unreachable dream.

But, wait! That very catalog of misery used as evidence by the pessimists contains evils that have been outgrown or overcome or contained to the point that they no longer flourish. Cannibalism and slavery – and we might add suttee, *auto-da-fé*, crucifixion, smallpox – are evils that, for the most part, *have* been overcome and eliminated from human society.

Even the individual resort to violence, held to be the hallmark of the sovereign state, has been generally eliminated as a permissible activity for individual citizens – why should we think it impossible to overcome group violence when we have already agreed to outlaw individual violence?

Furthermore, it is probable that war is a cultural, rather than a biological, artefact. So far as we can tell, organized warfare is only about 10,000 years old, while the human species is much older. And if we compare our warfare to the interspecies violence that some other species engage in,

> the specifically human cultural elements make the dissimilarities more striking than the similarities. For example: animals that fight with those of their own species to obtain dominance, territory, or females, always meet in 'fair fight'; there are never any fights of many against one.[12]

Common to both of these objections – that peace is undesirable and that it is unattainable – is the fundamental importance of the sovereignty of the individual state. So long as nationalism is dominant, we will indeed have motives for war, tendencies towards war, perhaps inevitable recurrences of war. One of the central themes of my argument, therefore, is: so much the worse for national sovereignty!

2 World peace as a possibility

On January 15, 1992, former American President Jimmy Carter noted that nowhere in the world was there a war being fought between nations – for the first time in recorded history.[1]

Now once a condition has been demonstrated as possible, there is no longer reason to think it is impossible; thus, world peace is at last a genuine possibility!

Of course, we have had periods of 'peace' throughout history – temporary and localized, to be sure, but sufficiently extensive for many individual human beings to have lived out their entire lives without suffering the horrors of war. Most of these periods of peace occurred in agrarian societies far from the European mainstream that all too many of us think of as the whole of civilization. They are thus dismissed as inappropriate models for advanced industrial nations.

But one, at least, of these periods of peace not only occurred in the mainstream, it dominated European society for 200 years – the *Pax Romana*. During that period and within that area, there were no wars between nations. There were, of course, occasional rebellions. There was nearly continuous border warfare. But within the boundaries of the Roman Empire, large-scale warfare was nearly completely suppressed. The second century especially has been described as one of the two 'relatively happiest which mankind has known in its long story of devastating wars and lamentable misfortunes.'[2]

How was this possible?

How did it happen that this one period, more than any other, managed to avoid the usual necessity of warfare?

While I am not a historian, and do not claim to understand all of the forces involved, there are two features of the *Pax Romana* that I would like to point out as tremendously important.

First of all, the Romans were a force for *unity*. When they conquered a region, they did not just rule by *force majeure*. They arranged for some of the inhabitants to become Roman citizens,[3] and they administered the area with at least some consideration for the local culture and traditional rights of the inhabitants. As a general rule, incorporation of an area into the empire made life better, not worse, for the indigenous conquered populations, bringing them the benefits of ordered civilization as their world knew it.

Second, the Romans brought with them and imposed (by political, economic, and eventually religious means) the closest thing we have ever seen to a world language – Latin. Throughout the empire the well-to-do, the influential, the powerful citizens found it expedient to learn Latin. While this overlaid language did not filter down to the common citizen, it made possible a level of international exchange of goods and ideas that had never before been seen.

Even after the empire itself disappeared, Latin remained as a unifying force in the widespread community of educated people and in the even wider community of the Roman Catholic Church. This common language was, together with roads and laws, the Roman contribution towards eventual, universal, peace.

Some have argued that our best hope for the future is a reprise of the Roman Empire in the form of a *Pax Americana*. Only the United States, they say, truly retains the status of a superpower. Only the United States is in a position to punish international aggressors and to break up international conflicts. And only the United States has enough moral stature to lend credence to its claim of acting altruistically.

This is not my view of world peace.

World peace, as Emily Balch said,[4] is not a negative thing. It is a positive spirit of goodwill and cooperation embracing all people as equally valuable. Such a vision is incompatible with *any* nation holding a privileged position or playing a dominant role.

Indeed, the next historically important period of peace after the *Pax Romana* occurred not through the dominance of any one nation, but through a consciously constructed balance of power.

Political developments in the modern era gradually replaced the feudal enclaves of the Middle Ages with nation-states that were simultaneously more peaceful internally and more fearsome externally. The key to war and peace came to be the relations between these states.

> In earlier times civil violence and territorial wars flowed one into the other and were endemic. From the eighteenth century the nation-state had the power, and the technological means, to preserve the peace at home and to wage, or not wage, wars outside. Wars were larger, more destructive – and fewer. It was no longer hoped that perpetual peace could come by a return to Christendom or by an advance to some new, universal regime. The system that made the century from 1815–1914 predominantly a century of peace was the system of the balance of power among nation-states.[5]

At first this balance of power was pursued by individual states acting out of self-interest, to prevent or to win wars with other individual states. Only gradually did the European nations develop the concept of the balance of power as an institution specifically designed to achieve the peace required by natural law.[6] But the maintenance of the balance of power between nations tended to advance and reinforce the development of the spirit of nationalism until it overwhelmed all other views of the state.

Many things contributed to the development of the nation-state, but perhaps the most important have been the technological and economic advances that were the forerunners of industrialization; the development of trade as a fundamental economic force; and military developments in tactics and ordnance that led to the demise of the walled city. Taken together, these and other factors made it both possible and profitable for central governments to extend their control over the countryside.

Now, nationalism has come to be the dominant political fact of our time. To many, this has seemed so fitting and appropriate that they cannot conceive of any other way of organizing the world – at least not in the foreseeable future. To others, however, nationalism has seemed to be the worst problem humanity faces, causing hatred, bigotry, violence, war, and, perhaps, eventual nuclear destruction. Obviously people are divided in their views on the subject, and '[e]ven among serious students of history and politics, nationalism continues to be a source of grave confusion.'[7]

The simplest definition of 'nationalism' is 'that state of mind in which the political loyalty is felt to be owed to the nation.'[8]

Etymologically, the word 'nation' is rooted in the Latin *natio*, meaning the largest group of cultural or ethnic descent (above tribe, clan, family, etc.), but not necessarily a political organization. Thus

> the Romans were following all earlier usage when they pronounced the Jews to be a *natio*, as also the Greeks and the assemblage of German tribes, because it was not as Jews, Greeks or Germans that they were politically organised. In the same way, they did not regard themselves, the Romans, as a *natio*, precisely because they were politically organised as tribes, as a city-state or as an empire, on lines that made the word irrelevant to them.[9]

Despite the semi-mystical appeal of the nation to scholars and jingoists alike, there is no *a priori* reason why our chief principal allegiance should be to a nation. Indeed, '[t]he evidence is overwhelming that the clan, the tribe, the city-state or the empire have mobilised the political loyalty no less effectively and intensely than the nation has done, and perhaps even more so.'[10]

I, of course, intend to argue that in the future we will normally feel our primary political loyalty to the earth-community, then, perhaps, to interstellar groupings of planetary populations into confederations, federations, or empires. We will look back on the embattled nations of the past as we now look on the tribal and feudal phases of our culture, as necessary, perhaps, and possessed of their own charms, but clearly a primitive condition that had to be outgrown.

A new possibility

But just as imperial fiat is not the only possible order, an enforced peace is not the only form of peace, and the nation-state is not the only form of political organization. I believe we are finally entering an era when the long-held dream of world peace can be realized by the practical efforts of world citizens, acting *as* citizens of the world. As Kant said:

> Since the narrower or wider community of the peoples of the earth has developed so far that a violation of rights in one place is felt throughout the world, the idea of a law of world citizenship is no high-flown or exaggerated notion. It is a supplement to the unwritten code of the civil and international law, indispensable for the maintenance of the public human rights and hence also of perpetual peace.[11]

There are many reasons why the world today is different from that of the past, and many of these differences contribute to the prospects for world peace.

Rise of world culture

First of all, there is the rise of a world culture.

Primarily because of improved communications and travel, the people of the world are seeing each other more than ever before, and they are coming closer together in their values and social behavior. Rock music and the standard business suit may be intrinsically unattractive to many, but their near-universal spread has made it easier for citizens of different countries to see each other as being alike, as worthy of being treated the same. This diminution of the differences between us can be (and is) deplored by some as a loss of variety, beauty, and culture, but it cannot be doubted that we as a species are more likely to war with those we perceive as 'different,' and so the reduction of the differences between us simultaneously reduces the likelihood that we will go to war.

Those of a less optimistic bent, who are fond of seeing the glass as half-empty, are likely to point out here that the dominant trend in today's world is not towards internationalization, but towards fragmentation, nationalism, bigotry, and even tribalism. Some point with glee to the fact that the first thing liberated East Europeans want to do is to kill their ethnically different neighbors, and the first thing de-colonized Africans want to do is to exploit each other or return to tribal warfare. There is some truth to this, but not much.[12]

While one should reasonably be chary of grand designs and comprehensive theories in the social sciences, I believe it is useful, important, and intellectually respectable to look for general trends and progressions. I submit that a natural – not an inevitable, not a mandatory, just a natural – progression for the political structure of human societies is family, clan or tribe, city-state, feudal fiefdom, nation-state, international government, world government, interplanetary government, universal government.

The essence of this view is, as Dennis Ross once remarked, that 'Each level of problems needs a level of government to deal with it effectively. The challenge is first to create each level of government and then to restrict it to its appropriate sphere of action.'[13]

Governmental jurisdictions should overlap vertically, so that each level would have a lower level to deal with more localized problems in the same geographic area, and a higher level to deal with more widespread problems, but governmental jurisdiction should never either overlap horizontally, so that more than one government on the same level claims the right to make a decision in the same area, or be disjoint horizontally, so that two same-level governments have no higher-level authority to resolve disputes between them. In such an ideal system, there are checks and balances, local *and* centralized functions. Each problem is solved by the appropriate level of government, and each level of government relies on those higher and lower than itself to solve what it cannot.

Families, for example, cannot solve all their own problems. They cannot allocate grazing rights, build large-scale irrigation, construct roads, or protect themselves against marauding groups. To deal with these problems they need some higher authority, some greater unity for collective action.

Clans and tribes served (and still serve) to meet these needs for many human beings. It is no longer fashionable to refer to these people as 'primitive'; rather, we are told that 'their culture is not necessarily less advanced, it is just different – they have chosen a different way of life and we should respect it.' Now clearly my conception of a 'natural' progression implies that such tribes *are* primitive (with respect to us, just as we are 'primitive' with respect to the hoped-for world civilization of the future).

This is not in any way a denigration of the *people* involved. (I happened to be born into a somewhat primitive culture myself; I do not feel the least bit inferior to the Queen of England *as a result of the fact of the society into which I was born*, though she may well be, for example, more gracious and urbane than I as a result of her own good luck and moral character and, to that extent, objectively 'better' than I turned out to be in the end.) It is, however, an intentional devaluation of their *culture* when compared with others. I believe that cultures of that sort are less desirable and can be seen to be so by employing John Stuart Mill's famous criterion: ask the person who has tried them both.

Like many of our friends and family, my wife and I worked hard to escape from the culture of backwoods Arkansas. When, in the 1960s, we encountered the 'back to nature' movement among the privileged scions of eastern urban America, we were bemused and a bit contemptuous. 'They don't know,' we said, 'what they're talking about. *We* know, and we want no part of it.' For the most part, we were right. The hippie communes and individual cabin-builders generally flocked back to civilization after poverty lost its charm. My friend Tom Kimmons is the only one I know who stayed in the hills of Arkansas, but he doesn't count because (a) he came from Arkansas and *did* know what he was getting into, (b) he is a philosopher and therefore smarter than most people by definition, (c) he is musically gifted and occasionally makes excursions into the big cities to earn a few quick bucks, and (d) he is using his organizational talents to bring some of the benefits of civilization to Shirley, Arkansas, without destroying its fundamentally rural nature, but he himself no longer lives by raising cows.

Of the civilized folks who have moved into primitive areas, almost none actually adopted and maintained the very same ways of life as the primitive people they lived among. Conversely, of the millions who have moved from primitive societies to more advanced ones, only a comparative handful willingly go back to exactly the same conditions as their mothers and fathers 'enjoyed.' The fact of the matter is, we have an overwhelming amount of empirical evidence that, given the choice, human beings prefer to live in societies that are more advanced along my natural progression.

Having said all that, how am I to account for the apparent reversion to nationalism and tribalism in the world today?

The general answer is that you have to walk before you can run. Most societies need to progress through something like these stages in something like the stated order – when they are artificially forced into an inappropriate stage, trouble will result.

In the case of Eastern Europe, it seems clear that, whether or not Russia was ever a nation-state, the Union of Soviet Socialist Republics never was either a nation-state or a voluntary international federation. Those 'countries' that are left in the wreckage of the USSR lost the chance to develop their own national identity. Now, having rejected the artificial nationhood of the USSR, they are trying to build or rebuild nations in weeks or months, before they heal the antagonisms of decades and centuries.

The solution to this kind of problem is to impose order, allow political fragmentation to occur, conduct plebiscites at the lowest possible level, induce irredentist or oppressed groups to move elsewhere by offering them land and financial advantages, consolidate workable governments at the lowest possible level, with international oversight of 'higher-level' problems until they form their own voluntary associations, and wait for them to mature. When they have solved their local problems, they will be ready to construct national governments. When national governments mature, they enter into associations and federations. After they have achieved their legitimate nationalistic aspirations, they will be ready to consider joining the world government.

Africa and the Middle East are a bit more troublesome. These countries, for the most part, do not have even the level of political and economic development of Eastern Europe. They bitterly resent the colonial exploitation of the past, for obvious good reasons. They feel deprived in two different, often contradictory, ways: (1) they feel they have lost much that was good in their own cultures, overwhelmed by the forces of colonialism, but (2) they also feel under-privileged *by Western standards*, and want the wealth, the education, and the conveniences for their children that are available to the wealthy citizens of industrialized nations. Many are acutely aware of these culturally dissonant tugs. They will end up choosing for themselves, and I believe that most will move towards the Western culture of individual freedom, industrial production, conjugal families, freedom of expression, and political democracy. If they don't, we should wish them well and offer our friendship without requiring that they become like us.

The more difficult problem arises when some of the population is not aware of the issues, or not empowered to choose. If a woman's culture requires that she hobble her feet, or wear a veil, or be subservient to her husband, who are we to interfere? On the view of the equality of all cultures (or of cultural relativism, which need not be the same thing), it would be wrong for us to 'interfere' in a naturally developed culture, even though there is no real sense in which the woman has chosen her life at all.

On my view, this is mistaken. We have the right and the duty to interfere, for example, in a slave-holding society, unless and until we are convinced that the slaves themselves genuinely wish to be slaves. Just because oppression is 'naturally developed' does not mean that it is morally excusable, and if slavery is not morally excusable, then neither is our tolerance of it.

The great power of the democratic ideal is that all individuals deserve as much control as possible over the conditions of their own life. (Incidentally, while industrialization may appeal primarily for its economic advantages, it too encourages personal liberty. In normal circumstances an industrial worker has more freedom and flexibility in choosing the terms and conditions of employment than does the agricultural serf or the feudal guild member.) If societies choose voluntarily to give up their right of choice (as Nazi Germany, Fascist Italy, and Communist China may perhaps have chosen, and as the fundamentalist Moslems in Algeria seem intent on choosing now) then indeed we should allow them to go their own way (within their own boundaries, of course). But wherever we are convinced that the people have not chosen the conditions of their lives, it is our duty to help them achieve that choice.

I conclude, therefore, that the solutions to the problems of the Middle East and Africa are like those of Eastern Europe: plebiscites to the lowest level; international enforcement of stability; economic aid; and subsidized, voluntary, relocation of incompatible population groups. Then we give them as much freedom as they wish, as much support as they ask for, and wait for them to achieve political maturity. In general, the forces of education, economic well-being, and social interaction are the necessary solvents of ethnic grievances.

It may be that these 'troublesome' groups will surprise us. Their long-delayed nationalistic periods may be less intense and painful than our own have been. If international peacekeeping forces prevent nationalistic wars and improved communications prepare the grounds for internationalism, these countries may have *less* trouble accepting membership in a democratic world government than will the traditional nation-states of the West.

Furthermore, it is likely that the 'problem' of the Third World, underdeveloped countries, and nationalistic violence will cause the Great Powers to recognize that their maximum payoff now comes from cooperation, rather than confrontation. If, indeed, we abandon the Cold War hostility that caused Great Powers to go around trying to make things worse in each other's sphere of influence, that, in itself, will make things somewhat better. If, beyond that, we all turn our attention from the threat of the other superpowers to the threat of the developing nations, the way in which the world divides into Us and Them may change significantly. Just as hostility between the superpowers has been the greatest threat to world peace for a generation, cooperation between the superpowers could become one of the most positive trends of our lifetime.

Increasing mastery of economic problems

Secondly, there is our increasing mastery of economic problems. It may seem excessively optimistic to speak of economic well-being when many people are starving, most are poor, and even the developed nations are in the grip of a recession. Nevertheless, only the most cynical or unperceptive of individuals could deny that things are far better than they were a century ago.

The combined blessings of technology and social welfare programs have eased the desperate plight of billions of human beings. What has been accomplished in Russia, China, Europe, and the United States is nothing short of astounding in historical terms. The grinding poverty of serfs, slaves, and servants has not been replaced by universally admired forms of life, but none, I think, would go back to the old conditions. Indeed, those of us who grew up poor are far more likely to be optimistic than our liberal patrons, because they focus on the evils that still exist, while we look at our own family and friends and see, directly and unmistakably, that things are better.

It is written in the Bible that 'The poor you always have with you.'[14] In terms of relative poverty, this is a logical truth, so long as we permit any economic distinctions at all. But just as we have ended slavery and smallpox, we are in a technical position to end world hunger whenever we choose to do so. The problem is not a lack of wealth, but a lack of political will.

Growing political consensus

I believe we are finally beginning to develop the political will necessary to solve the world's problems. Conditions for world peace have been vastly improved by a growing political consensus of the world's population. Almost nobody of importance today seriously denies that society should be organized democratically and coercion should be eliminated wherever possible.

This has not always been the case. For most of our history, we were ruled by hereditary monarchs or the usurpers who overthrew them by violence. Now, virtually nobody is. (A friend once pointed out to me that future generations will find our view that Henry Ford, III, should have the right to rule Ford Motor Company as absurd as we would find the belief that George Herbert Walker Bush, IV, should have hereditary rights to rule our country – but that's an issue for another time and place.)

Throughout the periods of the two world wars, substantial numbers of the world's population were ruled by regimes that did not even claim to be democratic, but were proudly fascistic. Yet more millions lived in countries with a facade of democracy but no real control over their governments. Today, democracy is on the march everywhere and the consent of the governed seems likely to achieve universal acceptance (just as the consent of the married was once widely transgressed, and is now nearly universal). As people become more accustomed to democratic forms of government, they will feel less and less concern about being 'subject' to a world government, and more and more confident that their rights will be protected.

In addition to these general forces that have been at work in the world, two recent geopolitical events of great importance have increased the growing consensus that world peace is possible.

The first, and most obvious, of these events is the decline of totalitarian communism.

The importance of this change is so overwhelming, and the gratitude the world feels to Mikhail Gorbachev for making it a peaceful change is so enormous, that I cannot possibly do it justice, so I shall not try. Sufficient millions of words have already been written about the 'easing of superpower tensions' and the resultant decline in the probability of a 'nuclear holocaust.' All of this is true, and wonderful; paradoxically, though,

I believe this factor *alone*, while it increased the prospects of world peace *de facto*, reduced its prospects *de jure*. In other words, by reducing the probability of international conflict, the changes in Eastern Europe also reduced the pressure on the world to establish some institution to deal with international conflict. It made many people hopeful that peace would break out *by itself* and nothing further need be done. The second event, however, swiftly dispelled some of that optimism.

In August 1990, when Iraq under Saddam Hussein invaded Kuwait, the world was once again compelled to face the question of international aggression. The strength of the compulsion, of course, arose in large part from the importance of oil to the world economy and the industrialized nations' fears of what Saddam might do if he controlled some 40 percent of the world's available supply – but although the compulsion was new, the issue is perennial. Aggression has been a feature of human history from the beginning. Thoughtful people, and even practical rather than reflective leaders, have tried for centuries to develop institutions and procedures for dealing with aggressive behavior.

In the realm of individual relationships, aggression has been dealt with by developing social morality and governmental sanctions. The great power of the myth of the social contract is that it makes sense – *of course* we would rather that physical violence was the monopoly of a fairly predictable and impartial agency rather than the right of all. If any of us were actually asked to sign a social contract or to give up the protections of government, the response would be nearly universal contractual agreement.

In the realm of relations between social groups, however, this process has been far slower in its evolution and remains far from unanimity. There are even regions where the social contract is still primarily observed on the level of tribe or family, with the nation-state not yet clearly dominant. For the most part, though, contemporary legitimate physical violence is held to be the exclusive province of nations. The remaining problem is to overcome this use of force in relations between nations.

One of the ways in which the Persian Gulf crisis was illuminating is the relative unanimity of world opinion. While Saddam had some genuine support among the millions of Arabs and Moslems who feel oppressed and exploited, he had almost none at the level of governments and communications media. The problem, then, was to find a way to express and enforce world opinion.

The United States, in a typical action, pursued a response that was two-thirds military and one-third diplomatic, two-thirds unilateral and one-third international, and two-thirds motivated by self-interest and one-third genuinely altruistic. But as world reaction and internal political responses had time to mature, a general need for some legitimation of US military action became felt both at home and abroad. We said we were doing the right thing, but so did Saddam – who has the right to decide between nations?

In a rare show of near-unanimity, the United Nations Security Council authorized the use of minimal force to sustain the embargo it had decreed earlier. Almost everyone felt that this action at least increased, if it did not guarantee, the legitimacy of the actions of the US and its supporters. It is my hope that this effort will help to convince world leaders that it is both useful and important to have a world government. In any event, it seems to me to have increased, rather than diminished, the prospects of world peace by serving as an example of the recurring problem of international aggression that is relatively clear and unobscured by personal and national loyalties for most observers.

The aftermath of the Gulf War is also instructive. The citizens of the United States at first engaged in an orgy of celebration of their glorious military victory. When they sobered up, however, they found that Saddam Hussein – the personification of evil whose very existence was part of the justification for the war – was still in power and still oppressing his own population. Furthermore, while the Kuwaitis had indeed been restored to the political *status quo ante bellum*, it turned out that they were *also* not a democracy, but a feudal aristocracy without an overwhelming respect for human rights. With the oilfields of Kuwait ablaze, the children of Iraq suffering, and various ethnic groups returning to their earlier quarrels, it dawned on many American citizens that *even a victorious war* might not necessarily be a 'good thing.'

This realization, I believe, is part of another broader viewpoint that is becoming the object of international consensus: coercion is bad, and social relations that depend on coercion should be eliminated wherever possible. As Emily Balch put it:

> Relations which rested traditionally on a basis of authority and punishment have very largely yielded to an unseen solvent, an unorganized, unnamed moral fashion that has made itself felt the world around. I think of the relations of parents to their children, of husbands to their wives, of teachers to their pupils, of 'masters,' that is, employers, to the workers, of the church to its heretics, of the police to the populace, of penal officials to criminals, of the State to subjects or citizens. In all such relations coercion is less and less relied on.[15]

Insofar as this is true – and I think it is far nearer the truth than most people recognize as yet – we have *empirical* grounds for believing that the elimination of coercion is possible in human affairs: thus peace becomes a new possibility.

The growth of technology

One way that it has been thought that technology would make war obsolete is by making it so horrible as to be unthinkable. This has been said, in various ways, about the crossbow, gunpowder, field artillery, the machine gun, poison gas, and nuclear bombs. Nevertheless, war is still with us.

To the extent that weapons of war really are intolerable,

we have managed to eliminate them from 'normal' warfare either formally (as with poison gas) or informally (as with nuclear bombs). Nations and groups of nations have continued to use conventional military forces as instruments of national policy, with ever greater speed, effectiveness, and expense.

Indeed, technology has made some aspects of modern warfare *less* horrible and easier for the ordinary person to accept. The performance of the United States' military forces against Iraq, for example, was widely viewed (by American audiences) as being so effective, precise, and efficient that it seemed to hold out hope that armchair warriors using video-game consoles to direct high-technology weapons could seek out and selectively destroy those persons and mechanisms responsible for whatever wrongs we were redressing at the moment, without the good guys suffering any substantial harm or even unpleasantness themselves.

Subsequent evidence that innocent civilians suffered greatly from both the direct and indirect effects of our action, that Saddam Hussein, his Republican Guards, and the Baathist Party suffered comparatively little, and that the physical and political environments were extraordinarily favorable to this enterprise in ways they may never be again, have somewhat tempered the American people's newly rediscovered enthusiasm for warfare, but the overall political effect of the new military technology has clearly been in the direction of relegitimizing the somewhat discredited option of military action.

The possibility of a nuclear holocaust stands almost alone as a powerful technological goad to abandon war. Furthermore, as the superpowers move to reduce armaments and other nations subscribe to the Nuclear Non-Proliferation Treaty, it is quite likely that this motive for peace will have *less* force in the future than it had in, say, the 1960s, 1970s, and 1980s. If nothing else, the longer we survive *without* engaging in general nuclear war, the less real the possibility will seem to most people.

For all these reasons, I think the notion of technology-as-threat is not the most important role of technology in the search for peace. Rather, I believe that the most important beneficent effects of technology have been the development of the means of communication and transportation that are bringing the world together, converting us more and more into *one* society, rather than many, and leading us to recognize that other countries are full of people more or less like us who are entitled to respect and can be dealt with peacefully.

The second most important effect of technology in the movement towards peace, I believe, has been the development of space travel. Few images in recent years have exerted such powerful influences on world opinion as the pictures of human beings in space or on another world, and especially the pictures of our world taken *from* space, showing its beauty and essential unity. Together these psychological effects of the space program have played a tremendous part in developing the ability of national leaders and ordinary people alike to think of themselves as citizens of the earth, who are all in this together.

The third most important effect of technology, it seems to me, is the vast increase in economic productivity that has come in its train, and especially that yet to come, when we finally have enough robots to build the robots to produce the wealth we need to lift all of humanity out of poverty. It may well be true that our current inability to feed the world's hungry is a lack not of wealth but of political will; it is certainly true that wars are not always fought for economic advantage. Nevertheless, it is also true that it is easier to be generous when one has a surfeit of goods, and that nations seldom *initiate* wars when their populations are comfortably well-off. To the extent that war has been, or has been perceived to be, justified economically, the reduction of economic necessity through technological advance will reduce that element of rationality in war and make it a less and less attractive alternative. When you add to that the fact that wealthy nations invest more in education and that wealthy individuals at least sometimes perceive themselves to have more to lose in war than do the hopeless poor, I believe you can generate a fairly strong argument that increases in economic productivity reduce the incentive to go to war.

Finally, the one most frequently cited negative effect of technological advance has been the problem of pollution. Perhaps paradoxically, I believe that this threat to our individual well-being weighs in favor of peace (while threats to economic well-being, for example, do not). The chief reason is that many environmental problems are, in the nature of the beast, international problems that obviously require a concerted international response. They are thus a motivation for world government and, by extension, for world peace. In addition, while an occasional act of blatant disregard for the environment may inspire physical hostility (some Americans and many Kuwaitis would like to bomb Baghdad as retribution for the irresponsible and vindictive Iraqi act of firing the oil-fields of Kuwait), most do not. I have never heard anyone propose that the way to stop destruction of the rain forest is to invade Brazil, or that Canada should bomb Detroit to lower the production of acid rain. By and large, people who become environmentalists tend also to become internationalists and pacifists. They seek to 'think globally and act locally' to produce a better world for everyone, not merely themselves.

For all these reasons, persons interested in peace should support both basic scientific research and technological development in most areas, with confidence that the more human beings know about each other, the more they think of themselves as citizens of one planet, the more they are freed from economic necessity, and the more they understand ecology, the more likely they are to work for peace.

The development of international law

Yet another reason for increased hope in the possibility of world peace is the increasingly potent and sophisticated development of international law. True, there have always been formal relations and obligations between states. Indeed,

> International systems, systems of relations between states, may be traced back to the beginning of recorded time, even if this is far from being true of what we now understand by the nation and the state. The earliest extant treaty comes down to us, it seems, from *circa* 2500 BC. At one level, in its technical devices, the modern system has not been much more sophisticated than its predecessors.
>
> A treaty of 1278 BC between the Pharaoh and the Hittites incorporates practically every stipulation that a treaty might contain today.[16]

The kind of thing that we now think of as international law began to take on a genuine independent existence in about the middle of the nineteenth century, when even the powerful nations saw that international standards were necessary in matters of health, communication, freedom of the sea, etc. International commissions were convened and international standards established to govern areas of activity that required international cooperation. These early forms of international laws had the force of treaties, when properly signed, and the force of public opinion, to some extent, but they were primarily driven by the force of the market place and pragmatic rationality – if all but a few nations cooperate in matters of this sort, those few will be *disadvantaged* with respect to the cooperators, so the classic problem of the 'free rider' does not arise and 'laws' of this sort can exist without the necessity of an enforcement mechanism.

It was left to the twentieth century to begin the development of enforceable international laws, although the tradition goes back through history. There are two principal parts of international law that are relevant to our inquiry. The first is the effort to limit national sovereignty with respect to the relationship between the state and the citizen:

> Since World War II, the international community has moved in a series of conventions, charters, and international agreements from a position of strict interpretation of State sover-

> eignty to one that holds that individuals have rights quite apart from State X or State Y – an irreducible minimum in a sort of 'portable package,' which they carry around and which somehow inheres in the person. In this view, people do not lose these basic rights simply because they are temporarily within the borders of a State not their own.[17]

This tendency in international law is important for our purposes because (a) it constitutes a limitation on national sovereignty, which is intrinsically desirable at this time, and (b) it begins the development of the position that each of us has rights as a member of the human family and world society, not merely or even primarily as subjects of nations. Clearly these are steps in the direction of world government and world peace. But the second branch of international law is even more central to our concern. It is the long-standing historical effort to develop a law of nations restricting or eliminating the right of individual nations to make war.

Kant and Bentham, for example, had both called for a system of international law for the explicit purpose of keeping the peace. The dominant view of international law over the last few hundred years, however, has been that of Hobbes, that nations exist in a state of nature, as modified by that of Emmerick de Vattel,[18] that states are subject to certain aspects of natural law, rights and duties, without, however, giving up their sovereign right to go to war.[19] There the matter stood, for the most part, until about the time of World War I.

The League of Nations represented humanity's first great effort to establish a genuine transnational authority. It was intended to be far less than a world government. Its Covenant, for example, 'did not seek either to abolish the right of the state to go to war or to impose on the state the duty of resorting to war against law-breaking states.'[20]

The first genuine attempt to deny the right of war-making as a matter of international law was the Pact of Paris (also called the Briand–Kellogg Pact) signed in that city in 1928. This pact condemned and renounced the use of force (except in self-defense, or in enforcement of the Pact) in international relations. It was subsequently appealed to in the Nuremberg Trials and has become a generally well-established component of international law.[21]

The problem with the Pact of Paris, as with the Covenant of the League of Nations and all such protestations of peaceful intent and proclamations of international law, is that it had no enforcement mechanism. The first steps in that direction had to wait until World War II demonstrated the inefficacy of the League and the Pact of Paris.

The United Nations

In its original conception, the United Nations Organization was to enforce the peace between nations.

As a concession to political reality, the veto power granted by the Charter to the permanent members of the Security Council meant that the UN could not act unless the Great Powers were already on the same side, in which case it is hard to see who would be in a position to cause trouble, anyway.

The UN's first major 'police action' in Korea, while it might be termed successful (North Korea was eventually forced to retreat to its original borders), was a fluke because the Soviet Union's non-veto of the original resolution sprang from a boycott based on a different issue, and the subsequent prosecution of the 'police action' rested almost entirely on the military forces of the United States, with only token participation from the rest of the UN.

The UN's second major 'police action', in the Congo, was a fiasco that failed in its mission and nearly bankrupted the UN.[22]

If we view the Persian Gulf excursion as a UN operation, it would seem to be more successful. Iraq's original invasion of Kuwait was condemned by the UN; an economic embargo was imposed to force a withdrawal to the *status quo ante bellum*; member nations were authorized to use military means to enforce the boycott; several member nations did in fact provide forces to the Allied operation, though there was no pretense of a United Nations command structure; the operation was a military success, with Iraqi forces quickly ejected from Kuwait; the economic embargo continued, with reparations added to the conditions for lifting it.

The UN's record on the enforcement of peace is thus a spotty one, but seems to be getting better. The results of the Gulf operation, for example, suggest that politically isolated states may find military invasions of their neighbors to be counter-productive in the future. If the world community in general, and all of the Great Powers in particular, perceive an act as aggression, *and* if enough of them care enough to use their own military might to enforce that disapproval, then the aggressor is in for a tough time. Given the imponderables, however, it might seem like a reasonable gamble to many a desperate despot for years to come.

Many students of international relations doubt that the UN will become an effective world policeman anytime in the near future. Nevertheless, even if this be so, the UN has been and continues to be effective in building the structure and the tradition of concerted international action. Through its many agencies and bureaus, the UN has contributed to the improvement of the lot of many of the world's most wretched citizens. At the same time, it has been building a cadre of skilled and dedicated internationalists, and familiarizing the governments of the world with the attitude that it is a good thing to work together in international bodies. Clearly, the very existence of the United Nations shows that our time is more nearly suited for world peace than any that has gone before.

Decline of religion

To the distress of my mother, and despite the peaceful and pleasant memory of my late father, the Methodist minister, I must say that I believe the prospects for world peace increase as the influence of religion declines.

It is hard to think of any other single factor that has divided human beings, and set them at war with each other, nearly so much as has religion. Even the pious Immanuel Kant saw this:

> every state, or its ruler, desires to establish lasting peace in this way [by conquest], aspiring if possible to rule the whole world. But nature wills otherwise. She employs two means to separate peoples and to prevent them from mixing: differences of language and of religion. These differences involve a tendency to mutual hatred and pretexts for war, but the progress of civilization and men's gradual approach to greater harmony in their principles finally leads to peaceful agreement.[23]

Religious authorities assure us that this unfortunate tendency to mutual hatred and division has been due to excessive zealotry and other forms of human error and that Christ, in whose name many of these horrors have been committed, is really 'the Prince of Peace.'

Certainly there is a strong theological foundation for this view, and most scholars agree that the early church was in fact strongly pacifist in its teaching and influence. Still, there is another side to the issue. Peter Calvocoressi has argued that a militant reformist attitude is central to the Western tradition, which

> is a tradition which extols justice and *philia* (love of your neighbor) and insists upon the supreme value of the individual conscience. These are the things it sanctifies; it does not sanctify peace; indeed, justice and conscience are rebellious rather than conservative, disturbing rather than placatory. The heroes and heroines of the tradition, from Antigone onwards, have all been rebels and most of them have been ready to shed blood at the call of righteous indignation which, agreeing with Blake, they identify with the voice of God. This tradition was reinforced by Christianity, which is

one of the less pacific religions, and was then revivified about five hundred years ago by the renaissance of classical humanism and the Protestant Reformation's initial appeal to conscience against authority.[24]

Even today, while there has been a general decline in the use of force to save souls, we find that many of the continuing violent conflicts in the world are between religious factions. No doubt there is some truth to religious apologists' claims that the wars between Catholics and Protestants in Northern Ireland and between Moslems and Jews in the Middle East are not 'religious wars' in the old sense of being motivated primarily by religious impulse, but are instead the result of other social irritants focussed and magnified by religious differences. But the point is, without important religious differences those other irritants would not have the added effect of this magnification, and the level of conflict would be proportionately reduced. Indeed, without the religious differences there could be no discrimination on the basis of religion and one, at least, of the basic claims of injustice would disappear.

But whatever the case today, clearly many of the wars of the past *were* religious wars. Who would choose to return to the time when countries were invaded, leaders were beheaded, and individuals were burned at the stake *solely* because of strongly held religious views?

And even when they are not directly the source of interventionist military action to reform *other* groups, religious attitudes and influences tend to be primarily conservative in their social function *within* each social and national group. Thus, for example, when the 'religious' vote is appealed to in the United States, Ireland, Algeria, or Israel, it is almost always on conservative social issues and patriotic international policies – never in the interest of mutual respect and accommodation with those who are different.

It is probably true that, with the exception of Islam, few of the world's religions today constitute independent threats to world peace. Nevertheless, they divide us. A central claim of this book is that world peace will become possible when we develop a sense of unity in the human family. Insofar as religion tends to divide rather than unify, it is a threat to this process and I find its decline to be a genuine and hopeful sign of the increased prospects for peace on earth.

The decline of racism and sexism

One of the most heartening trends of the twentieth century has been the massive decline in racism and sexism.

Again, my critics will be quick to point to vast areas of inequality, extensive residual racism of the worst sort, and sexist attitudes so common that they are not even recognized as such. My wife, Doris Weatherford, for example, pointed out to me that Mary McLeod Bethune of the United States was the only black woman who served as an official representative in the meeting that drafted the Charter of the United Nations. Even those black nations who were beginning to win the struggle for independence, and who had overcome official racism to the point that they could send delegates of whatever color they chose, saw no need to share the power with women, and no one protested. Many still do not protest, and the prevalence of sexism in black organizations is as poignant and depressing as the frequent conflicts between blacks and Jews, who should be comrades in oppression if anyone should.

Nevertheless, to say that we have not succeeded in eliminating racism and sexism is *not* to say that we have not made progress. When you think of the way things were 150 years ago – only five generations, a fleeting moment in human history – the amount of progress we have made is astounding. Even in what were then considered to be advanced industrial societies imbued with the virtues of liberal individualism, black people were widely enslaved and women had little real freedom. The institutions of society, for the most part, either endorsed or ignored discrimination and oppression directed at blacks and women. No official governmental body can afford to do that now (as South Africa is painfully learning), and few individuals are both immoral and courageous enough to advocate a return to *de jure* discrimination.

The reduction in racism and sexism is important to the quest for peace for several reasons. In general, the concept of a good but discriminatory world government is internally contradictory, so the denial of personhood to any of the world population diminishes our prospects of success, and the elimination or reduction of those denials accordingly improves our chance for peace.

In particular, racism has been the occasion or excuse for many wars (especially colonial wars of conquest, and the subsequent wars of liberation) in the past. Elimination of such wars will not end all threats to peace, but it is an occasion for rejoicing.

More speculatively, one does not have to be a racist or sexist in reverse to notice that most of the world's wars have been started by men and almost all of the really nasty ones by white European men. 'Racial characteristics' and 'feminine attitudes' are two-edged concepts, and a risky business intellectually, but if the white males haven't been able to solve the problem, can it hurt to try a little diversity?

While it may or may not be true that women in general are more opposed to war than men in general, the decline of sexism and the growing emancipation of women has permitted more activism on the part of those women who do work for peace. In 1915, for example, the International Congress of Women was convened by Jane Addams:

> 42 American women crossed the war-imperiled sea for a meeting at the Hague in April, 1915. The conflict that became WORLD WAR I was less than a year old; Americans were not yet involved; and these indomitable women aimed not only to keep their nation out, but also to end the war.
>
> Addams presided over the Congress, and at its end, sent the delegates out to work for peace. EMILY BALCH, for example, traveled from The Hague to Denmark, Norway,

Sweden and Russia, where she met with foreign ministers and other officials, and she briefed President Wilson upon returning to the US. At a time when no national government had granted women the right to vote, the audaciousness and commitment of these women was little short of astounding.

Addams, Balch, and ALICE HAMILTON jointly published a report of the meeting and its extraordinary mission entitled *Women at The Hague* (1915). The Congress led to the postwar formation of the WOMEN'S INTERNATIONAL LEAGUE FOR PEACE AND FREEDOM and was a strong factor in the Nobel Peace Prizes that Addams and Balch each won much later.[25]

The increasing freedom of women like this to participate in the peace movement must inevitably contribute to the practical success of that movement. The elimination of sexism thus will be of great importance to everyone who opposes war.

Finally, the spirit of humanity that fosters world peace through world government is the same spirit of humanity that opposes racism and sexism. It is the growing belief that all human beings have equal metaphysical worth and equal political and economic rights. When all of humanity embraces these beliefs, the climate of opinion will be ripe for world peace.

Summary

Many, perhaps most, serious students of international relations believe that a world government is undesirable. A clear majority believe that, in any case, it is not attainable in the near future.[26]

Of world peace, however, nearly everyone believes that it is desirable, and a larger proportion believes it to be attainable. The reason for the large number of supporters of world peace should be obvious. The reason for greater optimism is that many theorists believe world peace is attainable *without* the creation of a world government. On this view, the self-interest of each sovereign state will more and more trend away from conducting military aggression and towards peaceful economic competition. Furthermore, the community of nations will be more and more likely to condemn aggression when it occurs and to suppress it through collective military action – not because it is wrong or illegal, but because we're all better off if we stand together against bullies and put them in their place.

I agree with this distinction between the prospects for world government and the prospects for world peace, but since I believe we will in fact achieve world peace through world government, in the interest of economy I will treat the two as identical and take it as the standard expert opinion that it is not possible in the near future to achieve world peace through world government.

I set myself against these conventional views for a number of reasons.

In the first place, as I have indicated, the historical trend is clearly towards larger and larger units of government, with world government the result of historical extrapolation.

In the second place, the logic of government is such that each level of social problems should have its own appropriate governmental entity. If something like this analysis is correct, then world government is a theoretical necessity.

In the third place, my conception of world government is less drastic and more democratic than most. Many who object to the concept of world government do so out of fear that it might be either excessively totalitarian (i.e., interfering in too much of our lives), or excessively authoritarian (i.e., undemocratic). Given my view of the nature and function of *all* governments, I agree that bad world government is undesirable. I might even agree that the current international system is so sufficiently developed that it is better to have no world government at all than to have a bad one. (This is unlike the usual case for situations of choice. It is better to have a bad scientific theory, for example, than no theory at all. And better to have a bad dinner than no food at all. On the other hand, it is better to have no spouse at all than to have one who makes you miserable. In this case, it is the tolerability of the current international arrangements that makes it reasonable to argue that we are better off with no world government than we would be with a bad one – in the absence of any order in the world at all, the other choice would be more rational.) But with the decline of both totalitarianism and authoritarianism in much of the world, and with the confidence that the mature industrial democracies would never agree to the establishment of a bad world government, I believe we should get on with the task of constructing a good world government rather than be immobilized by the diminishing possibility that we might make things worse.

Finally, with respect to the conditions for world peace, I have argued that the development of a world culture, improvement in economic conditions, the growing world consensus on political issues, the advance of technology, the development of international law, the maturation of the United Nations Organization, the decline of religion as a motive for war, and the rejection of racism and sexism all are positive and growing favorable conditions for world peace.

It may not come in my lifetime, or in yours, but it will come.

3 World peace as an institution

If it is true that peace is a positive thing, rather than the mere absence of warfare, then we will only achieve peace by building it. In particular, we must build human institutions that will guarantee – will constitute – world peace in the human family.

At the present time, no such mechanism exists. There is no human institution capable of effectively policing the nations in order to guarantee world peace.

The United Nations

The United Nations, of course, is the closest thing we have to such an organization. Its explicit purpose is exactly this. Some of its actions in the past have approximated this goal, and it remains our best hope for the future. The UN, however, is clearly not up to the task, as it is presently constituted. For one thing, the veto power of the permanent members of the Security Council guarantees that the UN will not be able to act in the cases we fear the most – the cases where the Great Powers themselves engage in warfare.

And even if the Great Powers agree that the UN should take action to stop some lesser state from breaching the peace, the UN as such is not equipped militarily to deter even the puniest of upstart nations – it has, essentially, no fighting forces of its own, but must depend on voluntary subscriptions from member nations to raise its forces and to provide the structures of command, control, communication, and intelligence.

For all this, however, the UN has clearly had an impact already in bringing the nations of the world together. For one thing, the mere fact that it does *physically* bring them together is an institutional achievement of great importance. The General Assembly of nations has the twin symbolic roles of legitimizing the existence of member states and of asserting the existence of the higher claim of the world community. When nations accept the principle that their actions can be discussed, debated, and criticized in an open forum of the world community, they naturally and necessarily pay more attention to at least the forms of human decency and legitimacy (and think how much better off the world is when everyone at least embraces those forms).

Furthermore, the various United Nations peace-keeping forces and emergency forces have been remarkably important agents for peace. It may be, indeed, their very absence of military capability that has made it possible for the blue flag of the UN to be planted between hostile forces, to fly over investigatory delegations, to symbolize the world's interest in maintaining peace and the outcast nature of those who violate the peace.

In addition, the non-military agencies of the UN more and more have taken on the administrative aspects of a world government – they coordinate and direct joint efforts of the world community to improve health, safety, education, labor conditions, and other vital aspects of world society *on the assumption that we are all citizens of the world*. The governments and individuals involved in these efforts, and especially the individuals they help, cannot but be affected with a new sense that important things are going on beyond the limits of mere nationalism.

World Court

The World Court, like the United Nations, has managed to accomplish a good deal despite its lack of the fundamentally coercive powers of national courts. The Nuremberg Trials were enormously important in showing the world that individual actions cannot ultimately be excused as merely following orders from above, and national actions cannot be excused as based ultimately on some natural right of nations to make war at their own discretion.

The United States, to its shame, has been among the worst offenders in disregarding the rulings of the World Court and hampering the development of international law. But if one can get past the repellent sense of smug superiority enveloping former President Reagan and his advisers, for example, in rejecting the court's ruling against the mining of Nicaragua's harbors, one must admit that the core of their argument is sound: there is no such thing as an international law superior to the sovereignty of the United States. This is a shame; it is something we should be trying to change; but it is a fact. If we accept the fundamental democratic principle that a government's legitimacy depends on the consent of the governed, and if we agree that it is an empirical fact that the people of the United States – *and the people of the rest of the world* – have not agreed to be ruled by a world government or this particular form of world law, then their position is sound.

I emphasize this point (indeed I overstate it, as the Pact of Paris, for example, *does* constitute an agreement by the United States not to use aggressive force) because it illustrates the fundamental *institutional* problem standing in the way of world peace: the persistence of national sovereignty.

We cannot have both national sovereignty and international law. The existence of law just *is* a renunciation of sovereignty on the part of those subject to the law – that is the whole point of law and its only hope of efficacy. It does not follow that nations must give up *all* their rights in order to bring about world peace, any more than individual citizens give up all *their* rights when they agree to abide by the rules of national law. But it is essential that nations give up their sovereignty in general (i.e., their claim to be above all other laws) and their right to disregard the judgments of the World Court in particular, in order for world government, and hence world peace, to become an institutional reality.

Throughout this book I will be arguing against nationalism primarily because I view it as an obstacle to a desired course: world peace through world government. Other critics of nationalism have found other, more direct, grounds for criticizing and calling for its elimination. Consider, for example, Carlton J. H. Hayes's view:

> Nationalism is partly love of country, but chiefly something else. Nationalism is a proud and boastful habit of mind about one's own nation, accompanied by a supercilious or hostile attitude toward other nations; it admits that individual citizens of one's country may do wrong, but it insists that one's nationality or national state is always right. Nationalism is either ignorant and prejudiced or inhuman and jaundiced; in both cases it is a form of mania, a kind of extended and exaggerated egotism, and it has easily recognisable symptoms of selfishness, intolerance, and jingoism, indicative of the delusions of grandeur from which it suffers. Nationalism is artificial and it is far from ennobling; in a word, it is *patriotic snobbery*.[1]

Grenada/Panama

It might be instructive at this point to consider two recent examples of armed intervention, both committed by the United States: the invasions of Grenada and Panama in order to reshape governments and punish criminal law-breakers.

Many supporters of these actions of the US government believed they were justified because they did in fact 'improve' the situation in the countries invaded. Others of course, both within and without the US, opposed one or the other or both of these invasions.

Some disagreed with the aims, preferring a corrupt and despotic socialist government to a relatively pure and democratic capitalist one. Even more disputed the facts offered in support of those aims: was Grenada really oppressive to any great extent? How did we know Noriega was involved in the drug trade?

By far the most extensive and important objections to these actions, however, were not that *they* were not right, but that *the US* had not the right to do them (especially since the US, more than most nations, has clung defiantly to national sovereignty and inviolability in so many other respects and forums). Indeed, the establishment over many painful years of the inviolability of national boundaries and the illegality of aggressive military force has been one of the most important accomplishments of international law – most would not give it up without some alternative guarantee of security.

But *someone* should have the right to engage in such police actions. No doubt a stronger case should be required, and intervention should never be taken lightly, but if a government is corrupt, tyrannical, and repressive, it should be possible for the forces of good to make it change its ways, or replace it.

Otherwise, we are accepting and perpetuating international anarchy.

The necessity of world government

Anarchy between nations, like anarchy among individual humans, is a condition more appealing in the description than in the reality. It is of course possible that both nations and citizens might become so mature as to lose the need for conflict, so rational as to view violence as impractical, or so moral as to renounce the use of force for any purpose. If these things should occur, there would then be less need for governments. (Whether there would be *no* need is, I think, still debatable, since even pacifists need roads, libraries, hospitals, and arbitrators.) It might be that nations will act as if they inhabit Rousseau's state of nature rather than Hobbes's. It might be that they will voluntarily cooperate to bring about peace and justice, and no individual will ever violate the prevailing norm of calm good will.

It might be, but are you willing to bet your life on it?

Better to align ourselves with Kant, who said in his 'Second Definitive Article for a Perpetual Peace' that 'The Law of Nations Shall be Founded on a Federation of Free States,' because

> Peoples, as states, like individuals, may be judged to injure one another merely by their coexistence in the state of nature (i.e., while independent of external laws). Each of them may and should for the sake of its own security demand that the others enter with it into a constitution similar to the civil constitution, for under such a constitution each can be secure in his right. This would be a league of nations . . .[2]

Logical extension of Leviathan

Suppose we make the effort to create a good world government, and then it turns out we don't need it, because of the innate decency of humanity. Where's the harm? We have laws that are never violated, and a police force that's never used. Peace develops organically, rather than institutionally, but it arrives all the same.

Suppose, on the other hand, we place our faith in human goodness and rationality, we take the first step through unilateral disarmament, and then we find out we were wrong. Too late! The bad guys win, and history is set back for centuries. The prudent thing to do, as diplomats and military strategists have argued for years, is to assume that we live in a Hobbesian world, make enough of an investment in military might to protect ourselves, and prepare to live in a world where bad things happen, but not as bad *surprises* since we are ready for them.

This is the chief line of thought behind the military and economic strategy of the Cold War. It assumes not only that nations occupy a Hobbesian state of nature, but that *no change in that condition is possible*!

Monopoly of force and control

Here is where I part company with the advocates of Mutually Assured Destruction.

I am willing to agree that nations inhabit a Hobbesian state of nature now (or at least that it would be imprudent to assume that they do not). But unlike them (and Hobbes himself) I believe that the obvious solution for nations is essentially the same as that for individuals – create a good government and give that government a monopoly on the use of force.

End to world anarchy

The logic of establishing a world government is *exactly* like that of establishing any government: we have mutual problems to solve, and we need mutual guarantees of peace and protection.

The principal reason that Hobbes (and, to a lesser extent, Kant) rejected the possibility of a super-Leviathan is that, in his day, the technologies and techniques of governing were not up to the task of extending effectual control much further than the boundaries of a European nation. The principal reason that modern theoreticians reject a world government is just the opposite – they fear that it would be *too* powerful and *too* efficient in its control of its citizens. If an oppressive nation is bad, they say, just think of the awful potential of an oppressive world government with a monopoly of force.

Hobbes, of course, is to be excused for his underestimation of what government can do. And modern critics certainly have reasonable grounds for suspicion of modern states. But we really have no choice – the only way out of 'the war of each against all,' where the life of the individual is 'solitary, poor, nasty, brutish, and short' is to come together in an effective, but not oppressive, scheme of government.

As Hans Morgenthau put it:

> Nationalism has had its day. It was the political principle appropriate to the post-feudal and pre-atomic age. For the technology of the steam engine, it was indeed in good measure a force for progress. In the atomic age, it must make way for a political principle of larger dimensions, in tune with the worldwide configurations of interest and power of the age.[3]

Who can punish criminal nations?

At a minimum, we need to have a government that is authorized to resist and punish any nation that aggressively violates the rights of other nations. If we could accomplish this minimum goal, we would have the negative aspect of world peace: freedom from war (for the most part).

I, however, do not believe that the role of government should be limited this drastically at any level. We also need the ability to punish those who commit other wrongs besides aggressive warfare. And, at the present time, no person or institution exists with the legal or moral right to punish criminal nations. It is not even possible, in the moral sense, to have a punitive war.

> War . . . is only the sad recourse in the state of nature (where there is no tribunal which could judge with the force of law) by which each state asserts its right by violence and in which neither party can be adjudged unjust (for that would presuppose a juridical decision); in lieu of such a decision, the issue of the conflict (as if given by a so-called 'judgment of God') decides on which side justice lies. But between states no punitive war (*bellum punitivum*) is con-

ceivable, because there is no relation between them of master and servant.[4]

The logic of the concept of punishment requires that the punisher be *authorized* to inflict pain on the punishee. Thus, one equal may enact retribution on another, or wreak vengeance, but no one can punish an equal. In order for criminal nations to be punished, therefore, a higher government must have the legal right to use sanctions, including force, if necessary, against nations engaging in criminal behavior other than warfare.

Now it would be both wrong and unnecessary for the world government to get involved in the business of lower levels of government: preserving domestic tranquility, protecting the rights and privileges of citizens, and promoting the general welfare appropriate to each level.

But some things *should* be done at the highest level of government. Preserving the peace is the most obvious. Resolving disputes is natural. Coordinating and standardizing is beneficial. More controversial, but I think necessary, is the right of the higher level of government to intervene when the lower level is guilty of misfeasance, malfeasance, or nonfeasance.

Obviously, this power is frightening to those who reject the notion of world government. It is not, however, intrinsically evil.

The power of intervention does not lead at all times to unnecessary intervention. Indeed, the only time the government of the United States, for example, has found it necessary to 'invade' its constituent states in this century has been to enforce the civil rights of its black citizens. Surely there is general agreement that it was right for the US government to do this, just as it is right for the Governor of Florida to suspend public officials at lower levels who violate the public trust. Why, then, should we resist the obvious parallel: good, effective world government is only possible by elimination of the sovereignty of nations, just as the US discovered during the period of the Articles of Confederation that good, effective national government was only possible by the elimination of the sovereignty of the states?

The practicality of world government

Let us take it, then, that good world government is a desirable means to world peace. What can we say to the claim that it is not possible (or not possible at this time)?

Perhaps the greatest obstacle to world government today is what we might call 'cultural conservatism.'

Cultural conservatism is the widespread view that 'I must preserve my way of life because it is unique and valuable.' The good aspect of cultural conservatism is its interest in preserving historical buildings, landmarks, documents, etc., and the sense of belonging it gives to individuals. The bad part is the overwhelming human tendency to say 'My way of life is good; your way of life is different; therefore, your way of life is bad.' This xenophobic rejection of otherness reinforces the worst tendencies of nationalism, religious prejudice, racism, sexism, and ethnic hostility in each little cultural community. It creates neighborhoods and regions where 'No black (or Serb, or Catholic, or . . .) better let the sun set on him (or her) in this county (or village, or parish, or . . .).'

Clearly cultural conservatism is an emotionally powerful attempt to cling to something important. Unfortunately, it is often misguided, because what is being clung to is frequently less desirable than what is being resisted (if the idea of progress makes any sense at all), or because it is not actually being threatened (it *is* possible for Roman Catholic and Protestant churches to function peacefully in the same neighborhood).

Cultural autonomy can be preserved

Cultural conservatism manifests itself in this arena as a resistance to world government on the grounds that it will threaten a local (usually national) culture. This may take the form of a primitive hostility to foreigners as not really people, but it can also be an expression of advanced and enlightened aesthetic sensibility.

For example, in the course of a recent European sabbatical I had the opportunity to attend an international conference of academic trade unionists. The delegates shared my concern for our profession and my dedication to developing institutions for the formal and peaceful resolution of conflicts. For the most part, they were similarly internationalist in perspective and dedicated to world peace. They were extremely interested in and generally favorable to the impending changes in Europe to be brought about by the economic integration of 1992. I was surprised, therefore, to find a strong current of resistance to political and cultural integration.

These professors found it obvious that most economic barriers between nations were irrational (though they continued a lively debate about possible exceptions, and the possible means of correction). Their chief concern, which appeared to be emotional rather than intellectual in its source, was a fear of the loss of national identity. They specifically did not want to become citizens of a United States of Europe – they wanted to remain Danes and Germans and Irish.

Now I do not believe that all emotional needs are irrational needs, to be eliminated rather than met. We are, after all, emotional beings and are likely to remain so for generations, despite the best efforts of Stoics to pursue *apathy* (the absence of passion). We need emotional allegiances, a sense of solidarity, and some form of cultural identity. So much is true in my friends' attitudes. But it does not follow from this that these needs must be met by autonomous nation-states. There are no *a priori* necessary sources of emotional gratification (with the possible exception of biological relations, which may be to some extent genetic).

I have been told, though I have not researched it, that if you ask children to complete the sentence 'I am a ——', the most common responses are gender-based ('I am a girl'). I suspect, though I have not counted, that if you ask adult Americans the same question, the most common responses are employment-related ('I am a banker'). The great danger to world peace is that there are regions and contexts where many such answers will be religious or nationalistic ('I am a Shiite'; 'I am a German'). Self-concepts of this sort are intrinsically divisive and establish ready-made hostilities to those who are 'other.' It cannot be in our collective interest to magnify self-concepts of this sort. They are recurrent sources of conflict and aggression and retard our evolution towards the human family.

But my friends at the conference were not hostile or jingoistic – they merely wanted to preserve what they thought of as their 'cultural identity.' Now, just what kind of thing is this cultural identity, and why should we want to preserve it? Partly, of course, it is rooted in dress and architecture, and is thus far unproblematic. No one has ever been injured by allegiances to *Lederhosen* or igloos.

Language is a more important and more difficult source of cultural identity.

Clearly our views of the world, our values – and thus our behavior – depend greatly upon our conceptual schemes which in turn are substantially shaped by our language. It is my belief that the maturity of the human race will not arrive until we all literally 'speak the same language.' (This Americanism seems odd at first, since our culture is overwhelmingly monolingual, but it serves as a striking illustration because it functions as an honorific for those persons whom we understand and with whom we can identify: 'I like old Charlie; we speak the same language.')

I will expand on the necessity of a world language later. It seems to me desirable and, in any case, inevitable. It will also, no doubt, seriously reduce the cultural diversity of the world. But it will not eliminate it, or even importantly threaten it, for two reasons. First, there is always the possibility of bilingualism. If the Danes really value their language, if the French remain convinced that no other tongue is simultaneously so graceful and precise, they will have the option of preserving their native tongue as an important part of their regional culture. I must say that I do not believe this will happen and that in fact I think mutually incomprehensible local dialects are both silly and offensive, but I think the same of many things I tolerate in others, such as *haute couture* and sauerkraut. If they care to preserve their local languages, the existence of a world language will not make it impossible.

But the more important reason that I claim that even a single world language will not destroy cultural differences is that, demonstrably, the common language spoken in the many English-speaking parts of the world has not done so. An Irish farmer, a Bahamian fisherman, an American cowboy have vastly different cultures, though they speak (very nearly) the same language.

I conclude, therefore, that to the extent that cultural diversity is good and worth preserving it will not be threatened by a world language or a world government.

Finally, I pointed out to my colleagues that a cultural identity need not be closely localized. 'You are already,' I said, 'Europeans to us and to most of the world.' Asians and Africans may see clearly the differences between one of their neighboring states and another, but the differences between British, French, and German Europeans are scarcely important. In my own case, I do not believe that my cultural identity is diminished because it is rooted in 'united states' rather than 'divided states.' No doubt a century or two ago my self-image would have been largely shaped by the fact that I am a Floridian (it still is, to some extent). And no doubt it was very painful for Floridians to lose that important part of their self-image through a bloody and awful Civil War, and no doubt they felt that loss keenly and believed that that part of their cultural identity was worth fighting and dying for, but *I* do not feel the loss. My cultural identity now is as an American more than as a Floridian – so what? In a few hundred years, French citizens will find it incomprehensible that they might ever go to war with German citizens, not because they have *lost* the sense of identification and solidarity with their fellow French, but because they have *gained* a sense of identification and solidarity with the Germans. Their world will be changed in many other ways, no doubt, but *this* change will not only not be for the worse, it cannot even properly be described as a *loss* of cultural identity – in general, cultural identity cannot disappear, it can only change.

Economic and cultural interchange will increase

Still, it cannot be doubted that an effective world government will accelerate cultural change. Reduction of the importance of national boundaries will facilitate travel and trade. Standardized formats and regulations will improve communication. Ideas and fads will sweep the globe in days rather than months.

One monetary system

It is inevitable that there will be one world monetary system.

As part of my American cultural heritage, I am perhaps overly inclined to think of all change as progress, but this change, I am convinced, is indubitably desirable.

From the point of view of the individual and the small business, elimination of national currencies will simplify the practical task of just getting along in the world. (It still is a mild irritation to me that my publisher thinks – and pays me – in pounds. To understand each other we have to do mental conversions. To settle formal transactions we have to look up a daily rate in the newspaper and get out the calculator.)

There seem to be only two serious arguments against a world currency: (1) it will reduce cultural diversity, and (2) it will eliminate one mechanism that governments and financiers have for dealing with economic problems.

As to the first, see above for my views on cultural diversity. We might agree to let nations print money (and postage stamps) with different designs and colors, so long as the amounts and rates are the same. I suspect, though, that most people will not want even this much diversity, because the practical difficulties and inefficiencies outweigh the aesthetic and cultural gains. There are other ways to make cultural statements.

As to the second argument, it certainly counts as a rational consideration, but to me it is far from persuasive. Instead of raising and lowering the value of regional currencies, one can raise or lower regional taxes. Or, better, if incentives are needed and justified they can be done by subsidy rather than penalty. When all calculations of value are made using the same universal monetary standard, the economy of the world will inevitably be more productive, which will be a social good. Redistribution of that wealth is a problem for ethics and politics as well as economics, but even in the purely economic sense a free market economy need not depend on differential currency values (as the internal economy of the United States demonstrates).

Substantial standardization

Other forms of standardization would also be useful and efficient. We can see from the lack of standardization of electrical sockets how much unnecessary complication there is in the world. Do English or Portuguese nationalists really believe their lives are *better* because they cannot use electrical appliances manufactured in France or the US? (I forget the actual European incompatibilities – my computer made me painfully aware of the transatlantic ones when I tried to take it with me on a wonderful European sabbatical.) Do American jingoists think that the tremendous economic cost and social isolation resulting from their rejection of the metric system can be justified by an appeal to patriotism?

To some extent, international commissions can help prevent such entrenched incompatibilities from being quite so likely to occur in the future. Of course, if the people of Switzerland consciously decide to reject, say, the standard railroad gauge,

I for one would agree they have the right to do so. They should not, however, just stumble into isolation without understanding the issue and having the opportunity to participate in a worldwide rail system.

The first round of standard-setting for television broadcasting has already gotten away from us, and it looks as if the US may be hamstringing the second round by insisting that any high-definition television (HDTV) signals broadcast in America must be backwards-compatible with the existing national television standard. One can only hope that direct-broadcast satellite television will be more completely integrated.

Space exploration

The final important practical issue I would like to discuss is more in the nature of a merger than a standardization – I believe there should be one international space program.

My chief motivation here is to get on with the job. As I said in the introduction, I am a strong supporter of the exploration of space and believe that no other single issue is nearly so important to the long-term survival of the human race. If we could combine the scientific, technical, and economic resources of the whole world into one unified program, surely we could move a little faster.

A secondary reason is economic. While I am willing to pay a much higher share of my income in support of the exploration of space, it does seem a bit unfair that Americans should have to bear a majority of the cost, and it is both unfair and irrational that the Russians and the Americans should have to bear similar burdens for essentially duplicative programs. Spreading the economic load would increase the resources while reducing the burden on those currently paying the most.

The third reason is cultural. When we build bases on the moon, and then on Mars, I want them to be Earth bases, not Russian bases or American bases. And if and when our ships encounter ships from another planet, I want them to say 'This is the Earth Ship *Mother Teresa*', not 'This is the USS *War Eagle.*'

The prospects for world government

I am convinced that an effective world government will someday be established. I have no hope of living to see it, and I doubt that my daughter will, but I suspect that my grandchildren might and I am almost certain that their children will. If four generations seems too short a time for such a fundamental change, remember that the United Nations did not even exist when I was born, and the first steps towards the League of Nations had not been attempted when my father was born. The Union of Soviet Socialist Republics, which my generation of Americans has viewed as the greatest threat to world peace, did not exist in my grandmother's generation and ceased to exist before my daughter came of age. Both the rate of cultural changes and the rationality of those changes, I believe, are at present increasing over time.

The United Nations

The United Nations Organization is, of course, our best hope for an effective world government. It is already an effective, flourishing, international organization playing an important role in the search for world peace, but it faces enormous difficulties:

> The organization has the task of applying the rule of law where no law is. It is trying to establish an international order in advance of, or *pari passu* with, the development of the law which the order must reflect. There is, of course, a body of public and private international law, but this corpus is neither sufficiently settled nor sufficiently extensive to provide the sort of base which, in a nation state, gives precision and authority and consent to the operations of those who have to keep the peace.[5]

Many of the problems of the United Nations would disappear overnight if national sovereignty were abolished – this, of course, will not happen soon, but the sooner it happens, the better.

The problem of insufficient funds need not wait on its solution for the abolition of national sovereignty – it can be overcome by a gradual recognition of the UN's importance and a gradual increase in the willingness of nations to support it. Eventually, a technological solution to the world's economic problems will, *a fortiori*, solve the budgetary problems of the UN, but in the short run, massive poverty, starvation, and disease throughout the Third World will continue to strain the resources of the entire world community. However, this problem could also be an opportunity for the UN. If the superpowers manage to reduce the intensity of the Cold War and lower the temperature of the arms race, they may look around them and discover that they no longer pose the greatest threat to each other – the militant poverty of the Third World is the immediate danger to both.

As the industrialized nations face up to the problem of redistributing the world's wealth, it is my hope that they will turn to the UN as the logical vehicle for the administration of this massive undertaking. The resultant strengthening of the UN's infrastructure, and the heightened visibility it will have in world affairs, should contribute greatly to its influence and prestige, and help smooth the way to eventual world government.

Many people think that the UN has been rendered powerless by the existence of a veto power for the permanent members of the Security Council. I believe, to the contrary, that this stroke of organizational genius, troublesome as it has been in the past, is and has been the key to making it possible for the Great Powers to participate in the UN.

It may well be that the veto will be the last vestige of national sovereignty to disappear. The United States, in particular, is unlikely to subordinate its overwhelming military might to the control of a world government without complete assurance that it can continue its veto for a time. On those conditions, however, we might well reach the point of agreeing that the UN is the logical body to decide on and legitimize the use of international force. Then, over time, as trust improves and war recedes from the world stage, as underdeveloped nations attain political maturity and economic security, it will eventually be possible to complete the democratization of the UN.

(Historical aside: The US Senate has long been a bastion of residual 'states' rights' in the United States. As part of that syndrome, the Senate has included in its Rules the right of unlimited debate so that any individual senator or small group thereof could prevent action on any piece of legislation by 'filibustering' – talking without end until the motion is withdrawn. Only in recent years has this effective individual veto been somewhat restricted – now a 'cloture' vote of an extraordinary majority can close debate on an item. Perhaps some such phasing out of the veto will be acceptable to all sides in the international arena, eventually.)

The rise of the European Community

It may be that we must pass through an intermediate stage on the way to world government and the human family.

Such a stage would see the gradual coalescing of the world's nations into super-nations, of which the prototype will be the European Community. (Already the constituent republics of the former USSR are discussing, even as they assert independence, the EC as a prototype for how they conceive of their future relationship in the Commonwealth of Independent States.)

The notion of supranational communities is not new in Europe, going back at least to the Aetolian and Achaean Leagues of Ancient Greece.[6] Various subsequent leagues and empires have periodically united and divided Europe, but what may well be the first step in the actual unification of Europe took place with the signing of the Treaty of Rome on

March 25, 1957. A clear line of succession passes from the European Economic Community established by that treaty to the European Community and Parliament of Europe that may yet lead to political unification.

No doubt the majority of Europeans are still opposed to the existence of a United States of Europe in place of their traditional national sovereignty. But the economic unification of 1992, the growing importance of the Council of Ministers and European Parliament, and the irreversible cultural unification of Europe may well overcome their reluctance within a generation or two. If that happens, and if a united Europe achieves economic prosperity and political stature surpassing that of America and the former USSR, there will be a great incentive for other nations to unite as well.

Already we have the first steps towards a free trade zone in North America. The unification of Africa is so logical that one wonders why it hasn't happened yet. Moslem and/or Arab unity may finally be achieved, and Japan will presumably be the center of an Asian/Pacific entity.

Theorists who believe this will come to pass are, for the most part, merely extrapolating historical tendencies. City-states and feudal fiefdoms could not compete with modern nations, so they were willy-nilly forced to unite. Unification proceeded generally along lines of geographical, linguistic, and cultural similarities, in more or less that order of precedence. Modern states completed that process some 200 years ago, and nationalism has been the dominant mode since then. Both Hobbes and Kant believed that, whatever the intrinsic desirability of greater unification, physical and technical difficulties limited the size of political units, so that supernations and world government were impractical and unachievable.

But the forces that impelled us to national unity will not stop there, and technical progress means that unification no longer has to stop there. Since the Spartans and Athenians have overcome their cultural separation, the Swiss and Belgians have risen above internal language differences, and the

Chinese have mastered vast stretches of geography, there no longer seem to be insuperable bars to European unity. Indeed, as we shall see below, national independence is quickly being replaced by international interdependence. Economic, technological, and environmental factors more and more expose the antiquated inefficiency of the existing system of nations. French and British veterans of the world wars may rail against the 'Huns' until they die, but they will die, and their children and grandchildren will watch European television, travel freely throughout Europe, spend European currency, follow the actions of the European Parliament, and become, culturally and politically, primarily European and only secondarily French and British.

Such a change is wrenching for an individual and stressful for a transitional society, but it has happened before and will happen again and again until it reaches its logical limit, the political unity of all sapient beings.

The decline of the USSR

No one who writes optimistically about the prospects of internationalism can fail to take pause at the disintegration of the Union of Soviet Socialist Republics. American jingoists and emotional nationalists of all stripes rejoice in the triumph of freedom and nationalistic heroism over the evils of international communism. To some extent, they are right, and I too value freedom over internationalism – if I have to choose, I would rather be a free citizen of a small principality than an oppressed citizen of a cosmopolitan super-state. The dilemma, however, is a false one.

Part of the decline of the USSR is a result of economic ideology. While I have some fairly strong economic views, I believe that nothing fundamental in my argument depends on those views. As it happens, I believe that the economic system of world society will be a mixture of capitalist opportunity and socialist security, but nothing important turns on the exact proportion of the mix. So long as we live under the traditional constraints of moderate economic scarcity, we will need to work and to participate in some form of economic exchange. And the logic of economics is overwhelmingly in favor of large political unities with considerable devolution of power to lower levels – exactly the political structure I foresee for the world society.

The *decline* of the USSR is indeed in large part economic. The *disgrace* of the USSR has been its internal political repression. The *disintegration* of the USSR is because it has never, in fact, been a legitimate nation. A legitimate nation, I hold with Locke, derives its legitimacy from the consent of the governed. Most of the nationalist groups that eventually separated from the USSR did not, historically, and do not, currently, consent to be governed from Moscow. Some of them still seek complete independence, and we should support their right to do so. Most of them, however, have chosen to unite with Russia in the Commonwealth of Independent States.

The essential first goal is to construct a political structure that the majority of the citizens of the former USSR do in fact consent to. The essential second goal is to achieve as much personal liberty as possible for those citizens. The third goal, which may have to be chronologically prior to the second, is to revitalize the economy of the affected areas. (Again, it makes little difference what theoretical basis the economic system has, so long as it works.) After these three goals have been accomplished, the citizens of this area can consolidate their gains, develop economic and emotional security, extend their participation in world culture, and gradually prepare to transcend their hard-won national existence.

English as the world language

As I shall argue more extensively in Chapter 8, I believe that the prospect of world government will be greatly enhanced by the gradual development of a global language. As it happens, I believe that English will be that language, but just as it doesn't matter what side of the road we drive on so long as we all drive on the same side, it doesn't matter (much) what language we speak so long as we all speak the same language.

The shift to a common language will be driven primarily by cultural and economic forces, but it will grow symbiotically with political unity, as more and more of the world's diplomats and international citizens will be expected to speak English, and will. Many have noted how strongly national boundaries tend to correlate with linguistic groupings. This is not inevitable (as Belgium and Switzerland attest) and can be overcome (as China has gradually supplanted its many dialects with a common language), but certainly it is a significant factor in any process of unification. I believe that the emergence of English as the world language is a very important stage in our progress towards world government for the human family.

Objections to world government

Historically, there seem to have been four main objections to world government:

1. It cannot work for practical reasons.
2. It cannot work for emotional reasons.
3. It should not work for emotional reasons.
4. It should not work for political reasons.

I will address each of these in turn.

The first, which most impressed Hobbes and Kant, is today the least powerful argument against world government. No doubt it would have been impossible to have a world government before worldwide travel and communication were practical, but this is no longer a problem. (One night as I was working on this book I was watching, live, a debate in the Russian Parliament. A Russian journalist remarked that when he returned to New York in the middle of the attempted coup against Gorbachev, he learned more about what was going on in Russia from the free international news media than he had been able to learn in Moscow itself.)

An effective world government today would have more immediate and complete communications with all of its citizens than did the King of France or the Emperor of Japan at the height of nationalism. The real problem in this area is just the opposite – a world government might be *too* effective and efficient, an objection we will take up last.

The second objection is very powerful. There cannot be a world government, it is said, because human beings are so attached to nationalism they will never give it up, no matter what economists and philosophers recommend. If you combine this attachment with the very great fear and insecurity generated by the thought of losing the traditional protection of national sovereignty you get a potent force indeed. Louis L. Snyder has argued persuasively that it is this emotional combination of attachment and insecurity that brought down the macro-nationalisms of the past – 'Pan-Germanism, Pan-Slavism, Pan-Europeanism, Pan-Africanism, Pan-Asianism . . . [and] Pan-Americanism.'[7] But surely the same emotional attachment has always been felt for the dominant political unit, whether it be the tribe, clan, *polis*, duchy, or state. There is no *a priori* reason why such sentiments should attach primarily to the nation – indeed we are quite certain that at one time they did not. Why, then, should we believe the process must stop here?

It seems to me that the empirical evidence in favor of this objection includes the failures of the macro-nationalisms Snyder discusses, the demise of the League of Nations, the relative impotence of the United Nations Organization, and perhaps the fall of the Roman Empire. In each case, transnational structures failed to meet their goals and endure, and in each case except the last, nationalism was the principal obstacle to success. If we do a simple straight-line extrapolation from this evidence, we will conclude that internationalism will always be overcome by nationalism.

But straight-line projections are notoriously unreliable. (Consider the chicken, who comes to expect the farmer to bring food at the same time every day, until one day he brings the axe.) And the true lesson of history is that each level of political organization has in time yielded *to the next higher level of political organization*. Socrates' tribe was subject to the law of Athens. Athens is now a subordinate political unit in the sovereign state of Greece. Greece is moving in the direction of political subordination to the European Community. There are powerful reasons why the European Community *should* be subordinate to a world government. Emotional ties resisted each step along this path – some individuals are never reconciled to changes of this sort – but still the changes go on, as they must go on, until we have world peace and the human family.

The third argument against world government is the one that has most taken me aback. To my great surprise, some of my very intelligent, well-educated, and cosmopolitan friends have opposed the notion of world government, world culture, and world language, and have implied that I am an uncultured, technocratic barbarian for wishing to see them come about.

I have encountered three versions of this argument. The first, and least persuasive, is egocentric cultural conservatism: *my* culture is wonderful and should not be usurped, replaced, or transcended by any other culture. This version, it seems to me, amounts to nothing more than the natural human parochialism and fear of change and deserves no special attention. It just constantly surprises me that there *are* intelligent conservatives.

The second variant of the argument that world government is undesirable for cultural and emotional reasons is more general and respectable. It appeals to the great variety of cultures in the world today, the many aspects of beauty peculiar to each one, the enormous loss when any culture is destroyed, the variety and intellectual stimulation of multilingualism, and the unfounded audacity of white, European, male technocrats who wish to reshape the world to conform to their barren vision of how it should be. Thus, it concludes, not just *my* culture should be preserved, but all cultures, and world unification is therefore a bad thing.

Many threads of the argument come together here. Let me try to sort them out.

Remember that the central thesis of this book is that world peace is both possible and desirable. The secondary thesis is that world peace can best be accomplished by developing a sense of ourselves as members of the human family. The tertiary thesis is that both of these goals will benefit from the establishment of a world government (although I do not claim that is the *only* possible way to achieve them). Along the way, I argue that prospects for world peace and world government are improved by the development of a world language and a world culture. My primary intention is not to argue that these developments are *intrinsically* good, but that they are real phenomena that contribute to world peace.

Nevertheless, I do not shy away from asserting that the development of a world government employing a world language *is* a good thing. I believe that it will improve communication in ways that will reduce the level of confusion, inefficiency, and pain in the world. It will not necessarily eliminate all other languages, either. Since most Europeans are multilingual anyway, their only change will be that increasingly they agree to use English as *one* of their languages. Monolinguistic English speakers will merely find that their linguistic communities have expanded. The chief burden will be on Third World citizens who will have to learn a new language if they wish to have access to Western civilization. But if they *do* wish to have access to Western civilization, they will have to learn *some* new language, anyway, so they might as well all learn the same one and thereby learn to speak to each other too. If they *don't* wish to have access to Western civilization, they are perfectly free to continue as they are. It is not my intention to *force* anyone to change cultures.

Indeed, I think that cultural diversity is a wonderful thing, *as long as I don't have to be an agrarian villager* (I have tried it, and I don't like it – this general type of discussion might benefit if more romantic sorts would actually try it for a while). We are, I trust, beyond the point of classical European imperialism, and if we are not beyond that point, I am willing to enlist in the fight against it. But the intercultural problem of the next few decades is going to be just the opposite: so far from wishing that Western civilization would go away, the emerging nations are going to clamor for their right to participate in its fruits. Having achieved political independence, they will now pursue economic development. And who can blame them? If their cultures generate average per capita incomes of a few hundred dollars a year, would you swap places with them? In the interest of cultural diversity, do we have the right to tell them that they are not permitted to become like us? Would we be doing them any favors if we did? Isn't that just paternalism of the rankest sort? ('They'd really be happier if they just maintained their tribal patterns, but they don't realize that, so we must protect them.')

There are many and cogent grounds for objecting to the emerging shape of world culture, but that problem should be dealt with by seeking to improve world culture, just as we would our national culture (anyone who denies that their national culture stands in need of improvement is beyond hope).

There are also substantial grounds for preferring that national cultures should not be obliterated by the development of a world culture. To this end, I believe that world government will be relatively limited in its operation. It will primarily keep the peace. It will facilitate economic development and the redistribution of wealth. It will interfere in the internal affairs of a nation only when there is convincing evidence that the rights of some citizens are being importantly violated (e.g. it will not permit any nation to engage in genocide, slavery, torture, etc.). Individual nations (or perhaps citizens) will be subject to some sort of tax. Technological standardization will be encouraged. Other than that, Eskimos can live in igloos and Texans can wear ten-gallon hats if they choose – the citizens of the world have no collective interest in imposing cultural conformity as such. Indeed, an effective world government may be essential to the protection of some cultures from oppression by their *national* governments (the Meskito Indians, for example).

The third version of the argument against the desirability of world government for emotional reasons emphasizes the security and sense of identity we get from our national citizenship. No one, it is said, would lay down their life for Pan-Arabism, the European Community, or the United Nations. Yet billions of people stand ready to defend their national flags. This disproportionate attachment and loyalty indicates a deep spiritual fact: nations are central to our identity, security, and sense of who we are and what is important. To abolish them is not just impractical, it is wrong.

To this I have three replies. (1) Even if national identity as such is intrinsically desirable, that of Nazi storm-troopers, Russian *apparatchiks*, and America Firsters are instrumentally evil and should be eliminated; (2) a sense of identity and security is like a culture – it's important to have one, but it can be variously based on city, tribe, nation, or world; (3) giving up national sovereignty is not the same as giving up national citizenship – a citizen of Athens is not less of an Athenian for being unable to go to war against Sparta; a parochial New Yorker can be an American without ever leaving Manhattan; we can retain most of what is good in our national citizenship even when we become world citizens as well.

The besetting vice of the modern age is immoderation – we seem to be convinced that anything worth doing is worth doing to excess. Thus, some say, we are not liberated sexually until we are free to do anything to anybody anytime and anyplace. Or, conversely, politicians are unworthy of our trust if they have ever lapsed from moral perfection. Or, most relevantly and most perniciously for our purposes, a nation is not free if it is not free to do anything it chooses, whether to its own citizens or to other countries.

Throughout this book I argue that nations must give up their sovereignty, and to extreme nationalists it seems that I am selling their country into slavery, subordinating it to 'all those foreigners.' But what, after all, does international law require us to give up? Only the use of violence and death to achieve our ends abroad, and perhaps internal oppressions and injustices that are so odious they will be universally condemned by the world community. Is a country's perfect freedom to do these awful things so precious that we prefer it to peace? Why would anyone think such an exchange to be even advantageous, much less morally right?

It has often been said that nationalism is a form of religion. I say instead that it is a form of idolatry, for it is the worship of a human artifact at the *expense* of religion (which usually preaches peace). The sectarian pacifists were right on this point – to kill in the interests of the state (as distinct from the citizens of the state) is to commit murder.

Turning (finally) to the fourth argument against world government, we must ask ourselves if we really want to see such a massive concentration of power. Isn't it better, from a political point of view, to retain the checks and balances of the present international system than to risk domination by a government so all-encompassing that there is, by definition, no countervailing force? This fear is perfectly rational for any citizen of the world. It is particularly important in this case, however, because government leaders and military officers are in a pivotal position to influence the growth of world government, and they tend to be particularly risk-aversive in their assessment of possible actions,[8] so they can be expected to resist world government for what seem to them to be rational considerations.

Two kinds of nation have special reasons for being wary of world government: successful, dominant nations like the US and UK may reasonably feel that they are doing just fine in the world as it is, and any submission to the governance of others might seriously worsen their prospects; underdeveloped Third World countries, at the same time, might see world government as an attempt to re-establish the subjugation they painfully escaped through wars of national liberation. As my colleague, Kofi Glover, put it, 'You westerners ravaged our countryside when it served your purposes, and now that we seek to develop our own resources for our own purposes you have discovered environmentalism. You gloried in nationalism and even imperialism when it justified your expropriation of our raw materials, and now that we have achieved national independence you claim that globalism gives you a right to our resources. No doubt your ideas are good ideas, but they always seem to be better for you than for us.'[9]

If life were indeed a zero-sum game, so that every gain must be balanced by a corresponding loss, then concerns about short-term advantages or disadvantages for each country would indeed be of major importance. But the great advantage of cooperation is that it does not merely pool existing resources – it produces more wealth, security, knowledge, and happiness for everyone, if it is done right.

There is indeed much to be feared from a world government – there is not much that is *uniquely* to be feared from a world government. Whenever we agree to subject ourselves to governmental authority, we run the risk of being oppressed. It is not true that this risk gets greater as the government gets larger. Remember, a cruel baron and a tyrannical tribal patriarch had essentially *no* checks on their power to injure, maim, and oppress. By accepting the protection of Athenian law, Socrates ran the risk of being mistreated by Athens, but even when he faced death as a result, he still thought he had made the right choice and stuck to the bargain. Many nations have been oppressive and terroristic, but many more have not, and the historical trend is towards less oppression and more democracy. Finally, the degree of cooperation and goodwill that must be attained before a world government can be achieved is such that there will be little room left for tyranny.

Remember, I am not talking about world conquest, I am talking about the voluntary creation of a world government. For the most part, very few societies have ever calmly, deliberately, and democratically created a government that subsequently oppressed them. I conclude, therefore, that this concern is peculiarly the province of those analysts lucky enough to live currently under a good government and unwilling to take the chance of subjecting it to the devil they don't know.

Conclusion

I have set forth the reasons why I believe that the institution of world government is both desirable and practical, and I have tried to respond to what I take to be the chief arguments against my point of view. Let me conclude by returning once more to the general theory of government.

Every government exists to maintain order and provide benefits. Anarchists claim that governments are not necessary to maintain order, and libertarians claim that it is impossible for governments to provide benefits. These claims are almost unanimously rejected by citizens at the city, state, and national levels. Why, then, have they persuaded so many when applied at the level of world government? The objections that count seem to be primarily emotional and irrational, with the principal exception being the selfish but somewhat rational unwillingness of dominant nations to risk their dominant position.

There are problems at the global level. War is the worst of these, but it is not alone. The increasingly global nature of civilization must inevitably mean that more and more problems are global in scope. Some structure must be developed to deal with these problems. Voluntary cooperation is inherently unstable (because it cannot bind nations over a period of time), inefficient (because it cannot enforce compliance), and unjust (because it cannot overcome the 'free rider' problem and inevitably results in good people carrying an unfair share of the burden while bad people continue to be selfish). The only fair and effective way to deal with global problems is through a freely established, effective, democratic world government.

The logic of government demands it, historical trends point towards it, and pragmatists more and more are joining dreamers in advocating it. In the worst case, 'A force of all nations will come about when the disasters are deep enough to persuade even the great powers that that is the only way to go in the long run.'[10] In the best case, it will develop naturally and peacefully as increasing numbers of world citizens understand its necessity.

But in any case, it will surely come.

> We must tolerate and then learn to love the enveloping world we have made for ourselves, and we must learn to live in it with human dignity and brotherhood. Thus, we may be able to accept the ultimate in planetary thinking: the unitary nature of humanity on the planet, Earth. If the significance of today's instant communication and jet mobility has not fully penetrated our consciousness, the awesome pictures of our planet from space should convince us that the whole world has broken into the family circle and is not likely to retreat. Therefore, the family must let down its bulwarks and in diverse and transitional ways let in the world, in ever-widening circles, until the point arrives in the process of evolving culture when there will be only one great earth-girdling circle, around the family of man.[11]

4 The human family as an ideal

Depiction of the human family as an ideal to be pursued is far from original. Indeed, it is so common as to be nearly a cliché. 'The brotherhood of man,' especially, has been propounded in so many windy speeches that most of us are incapable of taking it seriously. And now that feminism is raising the linguistic and cultural consciousness of oppressed women, many have grown actually to resent the phrase.

Despite (or, perhaps, because of) its sexist connotations, 'the brotherhood of man' has been present in the official position of many of the world's religions. In the great Western monotheisms, it is a commonplace that God is our 'Father' and we are his 'children.'

Judeo-Christian tradition

Religious leaders in the Judeo-Christian tradition have made some genuine efforts to advance the ideal of the human family, though they have been all too willing to abandon it when the state required a justification for war or exploitation.

The human family has been an appealing ideal because it is a simple, yet powerful, crystallization of the vision that all human beings should love and support each other. For most of us, the greatest source of love and support in our lives has been our families. No other grouping in our society is characterized by the same degree of material and financial sharing, social and emotional closeness, and unquestioned and unvarying affection.

Most of the people in the world are able to love and support the members of their immediate families. Many quite naturally extend that love and support – even financial assistance – to an extended family of considerable size. The tribe and the nation are largely extensions and attenuations of this family-feeling. They consist of people 'like us,' sharing a common origin, culture, and collective existence. We are involved with them, dependent on them, obliged to them. We have a special relationship to them that does not obtain with those outside the tribal/national grouping – those who are not of 'the people.'

Clearly the point of the human family as an ideal is to extend to all human beings the status of membership in 'the people.' Much of the warfare, enslavement, conquest, and death in our history has been justified on the grounds that the enemy was inhuman, sub-human, heathen, or barbarian. We find it much harder to exert such cruelties on 'people like us.'

The ideal of the human family is that someday we will all love, respect, and support all human beings as we do the members of our immediate family. When that day comes, all war will be abolished, all bigotry and prejudice will disappear, and no one will ever starve or be homeless again. It is a powerful and compelling vision of how good life on earth could be if we could overcome the things that divide us and begin truly to help each other.

Many of our institutions proclaim this ideal. It is enshrined in our public rhetoric. It is advocated on all public and ceremonial occasions.

Still more striking, perhaps, is how few people venture to *oppose* the ideal of the human family. There has come to be a great revulsion for the horrors of Nazi dogma as well as Nazi actions. Even that most racist and xenophobic group, the Japanese, have learned that it is unwise to tell the rest of us about their sense of superiority (which was, in any event, chastened by their loss of World War II) or our offensive smell.

Hindu tradition

In the Western world today, almost no one denies the desirability of a world family. In the Eastern world, Hindu and Buddhist thought teaches that we already are – even more than a family unity – a universal Oneness. This tradition proclaims the unity of all of humanity – it asserts that we are in fact (metaphysical fact) all one already. The individual is seen as an artificial, indeed an illusory, separation of part of the unitary Atman from itself. Transcending this illusion necessarily leads to overcoming the feeling of separation of oneself from others, and to a practical view of the human family as one. Unfortunately, many imperfect Hindus (for example) are not yet ready to be at one with their Christian or Buddhist *alter egos*, but the theory, at least, is strongly cosmopolitan and unificationist.

A counter-argument

The ideal of the world family is so well established that I feel more obliged to present a counter-argument in the interest of balance than to argue for the obvious desirability of a world family.

In the many discussions I have had with others on this general topic, the serious disagreement I have encountered has almost always centered on the problem of national sovereignty and world government. Only one individual has actively opposed the very idea of a world family. That person was a friend of mine in the teachers' union who had grown up in a dysfunctional family. He greatly valued his freedom and independence, and the worst thing he could imagine was being forced to live with everyone as he had with his spiteful mother and abusive father.

No doubt a really horrible family *can* be worse than no

family at all, and an oppressive government worse than a peaceful anarchy. Likewise, a really awful movie can be worse than having no entertainment at all (for a time, at least). In fact, only of sex can we say with the folk-humorist Brother Dave Gardner that 'the worst I ever had was wonderful.'[1]

But I take it we can agree that such extreme cases leave untouched the general desirability of these things. Most of us wish our government were better, not abolished in favor of anarchy. And most of us would far rather live in a good family than not. As Eulah Laucks puts it:

> Only in intimate community can the deeper longings of mankind find some fulfillment. Up to now, the only instrument providing hope of fulfillment of basic human needs has been the family. Therefore, in this time of aggravated alienation, it does not seem likely to suppose – even considering man's technology-deadened sensibilities – that he will discard the wellspring of whatever reciprocal love he has or can have for other human beings. Some form of family is man's very source of meaning.[2]

Even the claims of independence can be honored in a good family. We understand that each of us has a separate life to live, that young birds must leave the nest, etc. Good families are supportive without smothering, loving without clinging. And, for those who would go it alone, it can still be a comfort to know that 'home is where, when you have to go there, they have to take you in.'

Much has been written in recent years (indeed, throughout history) about the 'decline of the family.' It is true that, in developed industrial societies, the family has lost its role as an economic unit and is yielding its pre-eminence in the process of socialization. But a majority still find in the family their principal source of love and acceptance.

Even the 'nuclear' family of modern social science has turned out to be more of a 'conjugal' family, with ties both forwards and backwards between generations, and laterally to siblings, aunts, uncles, and cousins. Although members of these families live in small groups, they continue to rely on each other for emotional and affectional closeness, and visit each other with astonishing frequency. Indeed, visiting relatives is the single most popular American holiday activity.

As, more and more, we manage to overcome racism, sexism, and religious prejudice, more and more we see developing a yearning for and rudimentary sense of global community.

The fundamental issue is not whether a world family is desirable as an ideal, but whether it is possible in practice.

5 The human family as a possibility

Despite the best intentions of earlier visionaries and social reformers, it was not possible for the human family to emerge as a reality before the present era.

For one thing, not since our biological origins in Africa has it been possible for anyone even to know of the existence of the several branches of the human family, until recently. It is difficult to love and treat as a member of your family an uncle if you have not met him; it is impossible if you do not even know of his existence.

The ability merely to identify all members of our human family is a new thing on the face of the earth.

Still, most of the good to be attained by the conception of the human family could have been realized long ago if each group had been genuinely willing to recognize and accept as family each other group that it encountered. No one would have known the entire family, but each region would have been peaceful and prosperous. That this did not happen is indicative less of a lack of intelligence than of a lack of maturity. We have always had sages, priests, and philosophers who have told us that we should treat each other as brothers and sisters – we just never wanted to do so.

Furthermore, a family, in general, cannot function without adults. Governance of the family must be in the hands of those who are both wise enough to understand the world and mature enough to subordinate self-interest to the needs of the group. Family heads must be able to provide for the family, so that it flourishes; discipline the family, so that it behaves; and teach the family, so that it matures. (It should go without saying that the role of family head can be filled collectively as well as individually – it can even be universal if *everyone* is a mature adult.)

I do not mean to imply that the ideal of the human family could have been attained if only we had a few mature individuals who were accepted as family heads. The characteristic concern, sympathy, and mutual support of a family is not enforceable from above – but if there are *no* mature adults to form at least a nucleus, the family will not develop at all or will be stunted in its growth.

What has been lacking in ages past is not a handful of charismatic leaders (to some extent, we have had that), but a general level of human maturity that would expand our fellow-feeling and consideration to the world at large.

For too much of our history we have been unable to understand our world or to provide for our family. Our growing modern ability to do both is simultaneously reshaping our families and our larger societies.

Perhaps the greatest change in families has been associated with the development of industrial means of production. The new jobs were not dependent upon the traditional family. Instead, they lured young men and women out of the traditional, rural, extended families and into the sinful cities. They offered individual freedom and demanded individual responsibility. The accompanying rise in individual choice extended to marriages, which more and more were based on romantic love and courtship and less and less arranged by elders in the interest of the extended family. The nuclear families thus formed had to live where the jobs were, and the jobs came not to families but to individuals, so the families spread out through the new environment.

As small, new, nuclear families replaced the old, more extended families of rural society, family values changed as well. In addition to the new importance of romantic and erotic ties between the spouses, young children came to be more important to the couple. Advances in medicine meant that a much higher proportion of children lived through infancy, so that it became possible for women to have fewer births and to invest more time and emotion in each child. The relatively smaller size of the new family made each such child a more important addition than it had been in the old-style family. Indeed, Shorter argues that the nucleus of the modern family was not romantic love, but the mother–infant relationship.

> The emotional web that was spun between mother and baby would reach out to envelop older children and the husband: a sense that the preciousness of infant life required an equally delicate setting for its preservation. Domesticity, the last of the three great eruptions of sentiment, would end up by kindling a cozy fire in the household – and conflagrating the community about it.[1]

For our purposes we need not decide whether the heart of the conjugal family is the tie between husband and wife or between parents and children – in either case, it is an affectional tie rather than a merely practical one. It is a tie between people who love each other and value each other's well-being. This is the familial attitude of our time, and it is this attitude that we need to extend to all of humanity.

Throughout history we have had isolated successes in parts of the human family. Many rulers have succeeded in disciplining their subjects. Some wise thinkers have managed to teach others. Political or religious leaders have united groups in bonds of oneness. And our greatest successes have been economic, in the rapidly improving ability of societies to provide for their citizens. In each case, however, the success has broken down.

For some temporary approximations of a limited human family, the death of a wise leader was enough to end a golden age. Others were unable to educate the populace and decayed from within. All too many succumbed to the external conquest that is always a danger in a divided world. At no time did we ever come close to a successful world family. Perhaps the best effort we have witnessed was the *Pax Romana*.

Despite its many faults, the Roman Empire was generally a good thing, even – perhaps especially – for those it conquered. Latin was the first good effort towards a universal language, and it enabled the most effective communication and dissemination of ideas that had ever been possible. No one would claim that the empire was democratic, yet it did consider the interests of those it ruled and was far less totalitarian than contemporary dictatorships. It spread what passed for civilization and did much to lay the foundations of contemporary world culture.

Ultimately, the Roman Empire disappeared. I cannot improve on Gibbon, nor do I think it essential to identify exactly why the empire failed. No doubt several different combinations of moral, technological, political, economic, and military weaknesses could have brought about its end. But the fact that our first real attempt at world civilization failed does not imply that all such attempts are doomed.

Indeed, the contrast between Roman civilization and the world civilization of the future may closely parallel the differences between the Roman family and the modern family.

The Roman family, like the Roman Empire, was largely a social and economic unit. It provided for the transmittal of wealth and power, the reproduction of the race, and the production of goods.

The modern Western family, on the other hand, has largely lost its economic function. Its economic relations are those of the individual worker, tied to no guild or family plot. It marries for love, not practical goals. It loves and nurtures its children, rather than looking on them as support for its old age (for that, it depends on industry and the state). It no longer lives with its closest relatives, but it visits them socially more than anyone else. Its families are united by affection and free choice (women now can afford to leave if they choose, because outside employment is available) rather than force, tradition, and economics. It is this free, loving, supportive attitude that distinguishes the modern from the ancient family, and it is this we should seek to extend to the whole world.

Likewise, the *Pax Romana* differs from the coming world government as the Roman marriage differs from modern marriage – the one is imposed, the other a matter of free choice.

Many arranged marriages have been satisfactory, even happy ones. Similarly, many conquests have worked out for the good of the conquered, and peace through a balance of terror is better than no peace at all. But one of those vast sea changes that has affected Western civilization may well have started with this fundamental feature of the family: romantic courtship – the right to *choose* one's mate – reshaped the very nature of our families, and hence of our emotional lives. As Emily Balch has noted,[2] we are everywhere turning away from coercion and towards freedom of choice: in our democratic governments, our abolition of slavery, our relaxation of censorship, our progressive education – but most especially in our families. Now that spouses are for the most part free to choose each other, or to choose to leave each other, we are focussing our energies on the rights of children to be free from abuse – a right that did not exist at all in the Roman family.

Perhaps the greatest changes in our family structure – as of our society at large – have been associated with the development of industrial production. As Shorter points out,

> The principal link here is the increased participation of young unmarried people, especially women, in the free-market labor force. The logic of the marketplace positively demands individualism: the system will succeed only if each participant ruthlessly pursues his own self-interest, buying cheap, selling dear, and enhancing his own interests at the cost of his competitors (i.e., his fellow citizens). Only if this variety of economic egoism is internalized will the free market come up to the high expectations of its apologists, for if people let humanitarian or communitarian consider-

> ations influence their economic behavior, the market becomes inefficient; the weak cease to be weeded out. Thus, the free market engraves upon all who are caught up in it the attitude: 'Look out for number one.'[3]

But women who internalized the principle of individual freedom did not thereby give up the need for affectional ties. Instead, they focussed their affection on their freely chosen mates and, especially, their children, and created the modern conjugal family. Again, in the words of William J. Goode,

> For the first time in world history a common set of influences – the social forces of industrialization and urbanization – is affecting every known society. Even traditional family systems in such widely separate and diverse societies as Papua, Manus, China, and Yugoslavia are reported to be changing as a result of these forces, although at different rates of speed. The alteration seems to be in the direction of some type of *conjugal* family pattern – that is, toward fewer kinship ties with distant relatives and a greater emphasis on the 'nuclear' family unit of couple and children.[4] . . . I see the world of revolution in family patterns as part of a still more important revolution that is sweeping the world in our time, the aspiration on the part of billions of people to have the right for the first time *to choose* for themselves – an aspiration that has toppled governments both old and new, and created new societies and social movements.
>
> For me, then, the major and sufficing justification for the newly emerging family patterns is that they offer people at least the potentialities of greater fulfillment, even if most do not seek it or achieve it.[5]

Thus the modern family, unlike the ancient one, values both love and freedom, and points the way to true world civilization.

Just as the fact that we have never succeeded in developing a world family does not imply that we cannot do so, neither does the fact that there have always been wars imply that there *will* always be wars.

It is fashionable to sneer at the American idealists who followed President Woodrow Wilson in describing World War I as 'the war to end all wars.' Manifestly, they were wrong. But the fact that they were wrong does not at all imply that 'the last war' is a necessarily empty concept.

Consider, for example, the case of war between the member states of the United States of America. So long as these states are susceptible of individuation, war between them is a logical possibility. In fact, it became a reality during the Civil War (or the War between the States, as we say in the South; or the War of Yankee Aggression, as the most die-hard rebels said). Yet I confidently assert that the Civil War was the last war that will ever be fought between US states. It is not physically or theoretically impossible; it just will never happen, given our level of cultural integration.

Likewise, war between the members of the European Community is far less likely today than it has ever been. Certainly, it is less nearly inconceivable than war between Pennsylvania and Georgia, but it is not something we particularly need to worry about, either. The steps currently being taken to formalize the economic and political unity of Europe are in part the creation of a new reality, and in part merely a recognition of an already existing stability.

No doubt economic efficiency is a major driving force behind the developments of 1992, but that in itself is not sufficient. After all, economists have known for at least two centuries that political boundaries and restrictions, different currencies and the lack of a common language have impeded the growth of trade and the development of efficient industrial production in Europe. But these merely practical considerations were incapable of overcoming the traditional cultural and emotional forces dividing Europe.

What has changed most importantly in Europe is the improvement in communications, the enormous growth in travel, and the increasingly cosmopolitan *Weltanschauung* of its people. They have come to know and to trust each other as never before. Their cultures have become more similar and familiar and less foreign and threatening. The spirit of the age has changed.

Probably the most important feature of these changes is the declining insistence on national sovereignty. While the issue of sovereignty remains the most important obstacle to complete European unity, it is far less overwhelming than it was only a generation ago.

What makes this development particularly heartening is that the countries involved are the very ones who have been *most* thoroughly nationalistic in the past. They have long and stable traditions of self-government, generally fixed national boundaries, and a strong sense of national unity. On the face of it, you would expect such strong and successful nation-states to be the *least* willing to surrender their sovereignty, and the newer, less united, countries of Africa, the Middle East, and Eastern Europe to be more willing to sacrifice what they have never really had in order to get on with building world peace. Instead, we have the puzzling phenomenon of nationalism declining where it has been successful and rampant where it has been frustrated.

But this is really not so puzzling. Most human growth comes in stages, and most human goods have a declining perceived value after they have been achieved, compared to what they had in prospect. We all must walk before we can run. We must achieve immediately vital economic goals before we can institutionalize generosity. We must have a secure sense of personal worth before we can reach out to others. We must, evidently, pass through some sort of nationalistic stage before we adopt a more universal point of view.

Thus the Slovenes, denied self-determination for generations, place that at the top of their collective agenda. When they have achieved the rights – and the respect – of independent nationhood, they will be ready to function in a larger arena. As we say in Florida, first you have to shoot the alligator closest to the boat.

This is why people of good will who wish to advance the world towards peace and unity must first be sensitive to the necessity of *breaking up* unhealthy – and especially involuntary – political unions before the pieces can be reunited into a democratic whole.[6]

To some extent, we have foreshortened the process of growth by making membership of the United Nations a virtual *criterion* of nationhood. No group feels it has been fully recognized until it is *allowed* to surrender the little bit of independence that must be conceded to the UN. (Analogically, individuals in advanced societies never really go through a stage of mature independence – their maturity is certified when they take on the role and obligations of citizenship.)

The forces of unity are at work, and growing stronger. Some of the forces are new upon the stage, and are helping to change the world. The forces of conflict and disunity remain strong, but they are the old, familiar, enemies: greed, ignorance, poverty, and parochialism.

For the first time we have the technological means to meet and get to know the other members of our human family. For the first time we have the economic resources to provide for the entire family. For the first time we have the moral, psychological, and cultural sophistication to resolve conflicts without the use of force.

For the first time, the Human Family is genuinely possible.

6 The human family as an institution

Many philosophers, pundits, and religious leaders have espoused the notion of the human family, but it was Karl Marx and his successors who made the greatest *practical* effort to achieve that end. Marx's essential insight was that the economic life of the social system could be like the social life of the family: 'From each according to his ability, to each according to his needs.'[1]

This simple thought captures much of what is best in communism – it treats social wealth as a common possession to be used for the individual and collective well-being of the community.

On the view of most contemporary observers, this idealistic view of human society has turned out to be a failure in practice. The reasons suggested as explanations for this failure are many and varied. I, myself, am inclined to think that the principal reasons were that (1) we are not sufficiently advanced economically – communism will not work on a large scale in a world of moderate scarcity of wealth; and (2) we are not sufficiently advanced in our social and moral development – communism will not work until other values have thoroughly replaced materialism at all levels of society.

Still, if Marx's vision has yet to produce a working social system, it captures nicely the economic relations in healthy families. These features are (1) collective production, and (2) sharing of wealth.

Most families have either a common enterprise (farm, store, small business, etc.) in which all family members participate in production, or a common bank account, to which all members contribute wages from employment outside the family. (On my view, when such sharing of resources does not occur, the unit is not a family, but a collection of individuals sharing living quarters for practical and sexual advantages.)

Likewise, families tend to have internal sharing of economic wealth. As a general rule, you don't have to pay for bread from the bread-box – you just take it as a right. You don't ordinarily have to account for small expenditures – the money is just as much yours as anyone else's. There are typically no *internal* economic transactions in a family (except for the training of children). Monetary relations within the group exist only because of the relation to the external world.

Life in such healthy families is characterized by the subordination of self-interest and an emphasis on the general welfare of the family. This is the vision that Marx had of the nature of a more desirable social system, and it is a vision that I share – not merely (or even primarily) for relations between individuals, but for those between social groups and nation-states. The accomplishment of world peace will come at the same time as the elimination of poverty and hunger through a sharing of economic wealth between nations, and we cannot be sure we have the one until we have the other.

The attempt by Marx's followers to accomplish his lofty ideals failed in part, no doubt, because of theoretical flaws in Marx's writings and in the later Leninist additions. But the principal source of the failure of the Soviet Union's noble experiment was not, I think, in economic policy (though that is clearly flawed), but in the social policy used to implement the theory.

Marx, you will recall, advocated democracy and believed that socialism cannot develop until a country has passed through a capitalist phase sufficient to provide it with a developed industrial economy. In other words, we must achieve capitalist and democratic goals *first*, before we pursue those of socialism. Otherwise economic strains always arise, putting stress on a system not sufficiently developed to provide for its citizens.

In addition, some theorists claim that socialism cannot work because its view of human nature is unrealistically idealized. It requires a degree of cooperation and a lack of egoistic greed that is not to be found among human beings.

There is some truth to this criticism, but I believe that it, too, is a fundamentally temporary state of affairs brought about by lack of economic development. When the machines have produced enough wealth for genuine need to disappear, what is described as human nature *will* change. As Captain Picard says on *Star Trek: The Next Generation*, 'We don't concern ourselves with such things anymore. We all have all that we need, why should we care about money?'[2]

In addition to the problems discussed above, I believe the most important single mistake that Marxists in general have made (and continue to make) is in failing to understand the importance of freedom.

While there have certainly been, and continue to be, many patriarchal and authoritarian families, they belong to the past, not the future, of the human race. The family of the future, both locally and globally, will consist of people who *choose* to belong, who *want* to contribute, who *value* the family and its members. To stand Hegel on his head, I would say that true obedience is only possible when one is truly free, and neither loyalty nor affection can be commanded. But whatever the merits of Marx's view of society, the one characteristic of a family that it does not capture is the need for love.

Families are not just economic units (although they are that). They are also social units, psychological supports, and peer groups. They are the basic source of our sense of self-identity and self-worth. When these values are promoted by praising and valuing all human capacities and excellences, our families help each of us to begin our growth to maturity. When, on the other hand, these necessarily high estimations of our own worth can be achieved only by the devaluation of other individuals or groups, then the family becomes the source and sustenance of racism, violence, and bigotry of all sorts. As Rodgers and Hammerstein said in *South Pacific*, 'You've got to be taught to hate and fear . . . It's got to be drummed in your dear little ear . . . to hate all the people your relatives hate . . . you've got to be carefully taught.'[3]

The human family will finally become a flourishing institution when these artificial religious and cultural divisions can be overcome and all (or most) of us can genuinely say that we 'love humanity.'

7 Economic interdependence

One major bar to world peace is economic conflict.

No doubt the cynics have overstated the case in their claim that war always arises from economic motivations, but such forces have clearly played a major role in creating the tensions and hostilities that lead to war. In order to reduce the likelihood of war, then, it will be necessary to lower the level of economic conflict. What is needed is a world economic scheme that is simultaneously competitive and cooperative, and one that fosters rather than diminishes the ties of interdependence and commonality constitutive of a peaceful world society.

Many there are who deny that such a system is either desirable or possible. Some, indeed, believe that economic competition can serve a peaceful purpose, by becoming a sort of proxy for war, while many others hold that economic opposition is a fundamental and unavoidable component of international relations.

It is my belief, to the contrary, that a cooperative world economic system is not merely desirable and possible: it is inevitable.

Already our economic relations are becoming less adversarial, as multinational corporations span the globe, and less fragmented, as trade increases, tariffs decline, and business people move freely from country to country. Yet, still, some resist this internationalization, clamoring instead for economic independence and aggrandizement, nation against nation, company against company, person against person.

One common argument for this point of view is the perceived need for each nation to preserve economic independence. Perhaps the most virulent strain of this attitude is the belief that a free nation must preserve agricultural production and sources of 'strategic resources' such as oil and minerals.

In response to this attitude I say, 'I don't grow my own wheat, why should Switzerland?'

It is, for one thing, both impossible and inefficient for any person or group of persons to try to produce simultaneously all forms of economic goods. Instead, an obvious principle of economic rationality tells us that any group prospers when each member cooperatively does the job for which it is best suited and shares the result with all other members. If Canada, for example, is best suited to growing wheat, replacing Canadian with Swiss wheat requires artificial economic interference. This inefficiency has to hurt someone: the Swiss consumers, who pay higher prices for their wheat, the Swiss taxpayers, who must furnish the funds to subsidize part of the inefficiency, and even the Canadian farmers, who find their natural market artificially reduced.

True, such economic inefficiencies are not *completely* irrational. They do benefit a few – most notably the Swiss wheat farmers who are artificially protected from competition, and the Swiss politicians, who receive the farmers' votes and financial contributions. Nevertheless, such policies inevitably lower the overall level of production, because agricultural needs are being met inefficiently. It would be better to let the Swiss make precision instruments, or whatever they are good at, and then trade for Canadian wheat. Thus everyone will prosper, as production and distribution are made more cost-effective.

To some extent, natural forces in the market place are forcing nations towards a more rational, less protectionist system of trade. As Kant remarked as long ago as the eighteenth century

> The spirit of commerce, which is incompatible with war, sooner or later gains the upper hand in every state. As the power of money is perhaps the most dependable of all the powers (means) included under the state power, states see themselves forced, without any moral urge, to promote honorable peace and by mediation to prevent war wherever it threatens to break out. They do so exactly as if they stood in perpetual alliances . . .[1]

A contemporary force for international economic interdependence that Kant could scarcely have foreseen is the growth of multinational corporations.

That multinational corporations are helping to bring about world peace may come as a surprise and a shock to the 1960s-style radicals who view them as personifications of capitalism's moral bankruptcy, but it is nevertheless a fact of our time. For one thing, there is the simple principle that you don't bomb cities if you own part of them; you don't seek to destroy a country if you have a large investment in its economy.

A second factor is that business accounts for the largest share of international travel. It is building, for its own purposes, a vast network of individuals trained to work from an international perspective, less dominated by the parochialism of the past. (It may be, as Marx would put it, that the desire for gain is causing nationalistic capitalism to create the tools of its own undoing – on the other hand, it may be the more prosaic fact that you can't do business with people without getting to know them, and the more you know them, the more likely you are to come to value them as people.)

A third reason why multinational corporations generally oppose war is that they have found that economic imperialism no longer requires militarism – the victims have all become willing victims, grasping at the opportunity to achieve Western-style affluence by selling their resources and labor at whatever rate they can manage on the world market.

Finally, multinational corporations must be careful about supporting war because, while jingoism might be popular in one of their business regions, the rest of the world frowns on conquest. Another Pearl Harbor would not only harm the export level of Sony Corporation, it would seriously taint the image of any corporation doing business in, or with, Japan. Supporting peace is better for the corporate image, and therefore for the balance sheet.

Not everyone is happy with the prospect of super-corporations ruling the world, though. Nationalistic forces in the Third World have recently tried to reduce the growing dominance of multinational corporations by various economic policies and legal requirements intended to promote local ownership and control. While these efforts have had some partial success, Biersteker concludes

> Despite the theoretical counterrevolution within international political economy during the 1970s, there are still a great many things the state cannot do within the constraints of the contemporary world economy. International constraints may have changed their form, but not their essential substance. The illustrations of the assertion of state power in the form of indigenization, nationalization, and national self-reliance demonstrate that although states can seize transnational corporations, they cannot control important aspects of their operations. It does not appear possible for a state to opt out of the existing international division of labor, even if it wants to disengage.[2]

For all this, however, it remains true that there is considerable opposition to economic interdependence in the world. Much of this is attributable to politically powerful pressure groups, advocating a narrow self-interest. This in itself is all right – that's what pressure groups are for, to express limited collective interests and advocate them in the larger society. Such groups are perfectly fine in their place, and help guarantee that the government considers all points of view and competing interests, with all the arguments pro and con advanced as forcefully as possible. Lobbyists and pressure groups play a legitimate role in a democratic society, but occasionally they have to lose.

I remember once, when I was the Vice-President of the Central Labor Council of Tampa, Florida, talking to a friend who was president of a typesetters' union. I asked him how his union was doing and he said, rather poignantly, 'It's dying.' The craft he and his fellows had been trained to perform was ceasing to exist, replaced by computerized typesetting. Their union was going the way of the Guild of Buggy Whip Makers, swept aside by new forms of production. In such cases, the special interest groups must lose – the larger collective interest must restrain them. The only other way is the Luddite alternative of rejecting all technological advances, and no one considers this a serious possibility.

But if the wheat farmers of Switzerland were *just like* the typesetters or the buggy-whip makers, they would have far less support for their current governmental subsidies. Their claims are not just claims to be supported for their personal well-being, they are claims that they contribute to the national security and the cultural identity of the country.

Those who justify agricultural tariffs and other subsidies as matters of national security concern say, for example, 'In case of war, what would the French eat?' To this I believe there are three answers, the first traditional, the other two new with our society, the three jointly sufficient:

1. If it is a just war, there will be plenty of allies willing to continue to provide agricultural and strategic necessities.
2. If it is a total war, the French will eat nothing – no one will ever eat again.
3. There will be no such war.

Never again will there be a prolonged war fought on the soil of an advanced European nation. Military technology has joined with political and economic unity to render such wars obsolete. Rather than continuing to prepare for the last war, we must learn that no nation can go it alone, either militarily or economically. Therefore national security must be integrated into world security.

Burgundy, after all, doesn't need an army, or have to have steel mills. And now, neither does France – it has the European Community and world society as a whole to protect it just as it has protected Burgundy.

There can be, then, no rational opposition to economic interdependence based on national security; what of the claims of cultural integrity?

Whatever you think of the *pronunciamentos* of Marxists and other economic determinists, it is indisputable that the culture of a nation is significantly shaped by its form or forms of economic production – a nation of miners differs from a nation of hunter-gatherers. And no doubt the romanticized single-family farm is a picturesque and valuable part of the cultural traditions of many nations. It *may* therefore be rational to keep some of them around as a sort of cultural museum and adornment of the landscape. But don't let's pretend that there is any *economic* justification for it, or that it is fair to cause other national economies to suffer in order to support such anachronisms.

Surely the most hopeful sign of the growth of economic interdependence is the development of the barrier-free European Community. In recognition of the inefficiencies imposed by national boundaries, a majority of European countries agreed to remove such barriers in 1992. If this grand experiment works as well as most experts expect, the gross economic product of the region should expand more rapidly and the conditions of life for its citizens become more agreeable. Already the nations of North America are moving in the same direction, and we may expect such trends to continue. It will then be only a matter of time before the world recognizes that barriers between such trade zones are just as irrational as internal barriers, and a free world market will finally come into being.

Not only will the elimination of trade barriers increase the well-being of the already wealthy nations, it will also attack the greatest economic and social problem in the world today: the need to transfer wealth to underdeveloped nations, where 'one-fifth of the world's population still lives on less than $1 a day.'[3]

Since many of the existing barriers to world trade serve specifically to eliminate competition from developing countries, in 1990 'Trade barriers in developed countries cost developing countries nearly $55-billion in lost export income.'[4] Elimination of such barriers will improve both the total efficiency of world production and its fairness of distribution. As this happens, the forces of economic interdependence and supply and demand will inevitably close out some current occupations and distress some social groups. But that, like the demise of the buggy-whip makers and the manual typesetters, is part of the price we pay for economic improvement. We may someday decide that the world is better off when millions of farmers use horses and mules to plow their fields, and we may use part of our future economic surplus to restore bucolic parochialism as an affordable cultural artifact, but to hold back industrial and agricultural production now, while millions of our fellow humans are starving, is not just quaint, it is criminal.

8 Cultural interdependence

One of the forces that is contributing to the growing possibility of a true human family is our increasing cultural interdependence. While it is possible to love and respect people who are radically different from oneself, there is no doubt that cultural differences have exacerbated international tensions throughout the period of international warfare. Accordingly, our chances for peace increase as we become more culturally interdependent.

A world language, hurrah!

Of all the components of that interdependence, none is more important than the development of a world language. Linguistic differences have divided us in the past, by making it more difficult to understand and appreciate each other. Even more important, though, is the symbiotic relationship between linguistic differences and nationalism.

> Among the cultural characteristics of nationality, *language* is, and always has been, pre-eminent. Anthropologists tell us that with primitive men tribal distinctions coincide with linguistic differences, and that the occurrence of two tribes with precisely the same speech is so rare that it may be regarded merely as a transient condition.[1]

Clearly, then, if we are to surmount the nationalistic forces that divide us, we must also overcome our linguistic isolation. Fortunately, we are already well on our way. I believe that a world language is evolving rapidly, that its development is inevitable, and that, on the whole, this is a wonderful thing. As I began serious work on this book, however, I found to my surprise that many people disagree on this point, some of them violently.

It has always been a dream of both idealists and technocrats to unite the world by use of a common language. The Esperanto Society is perhaps the most pure and idealistic example of this; the international convention on air traffic control the most practical and hard-headed.

The idealists and the technocrats (they need not be mutually exclusive) tend to cite the same reasons for their aim: a common language reduces misunderstandings, facilitates cooperation, leads to greater economic production, and improves the prospects for peace.

For our purposes, it is important to note that the notion of a family without a common language is almost incomprehensible. The level of interaction, mutual understanding, and affectional commitment we associate with the family depends upon close and effective communication between members.

Furthermore, it is a constant theme of this book that nationalism is a major obstacle to world peace, that it is both dated and undesirable and should be replaced as quickly as possible by cosmopolitanism. Yet shared language is second only to geography as a fundamental determinant of national identity. So long as the Armenians and the Azerbaijani speak separate languages, they will continue to think of themselves as divided into Us and Them. The rise of a world language will finally reduce this potent force of separation, and replace it with linguistic harmony.

Despite its obvious advantages, however, there are many grounds on which individuals have resisted the goal of a common language.

Self-interest

The most frequent, troublesome, and practically influential argument against a world language is that of rational self-interest: 'Why should *I* have to take the trouble to learn a new language? If somebody else thinks world communication is important, let them learn my language. After all, it's a lot of work to learn a language – what's in it for me?'

This argument, I believe, is well on its way to defeat. As a world language and a world culture develop, it will become obvious to each individual that it is both important and rewarding to participate in that culture. Of course there will always be some individuals and groups who opt out of any form of social cooperation, but when the principal avenues to education, political power, and economic advancement all require fluency in the world language, practical and ambitious people will come around out of the same self-interest that now holds them back. And when popular culture and entertainment become primarily available in the world language, almost everyone will adopt it as a means of social communication.

Language is culture

Aside from practical self-interest, the chief argument against a world language is that it will reduce cultural diversity, and cultural diversity is a good, therefore a world language is undesirable.

If the French were to 'give up' their language, it is suggested, their culture would be lost as well; if the Chinese 'adopt' English, they would thereby acquire a new culture. The cultures most affected would resist this process, it is said, out of an emotional fear of subordination. After all, if I 'have to' speak your language, you have 'conquered' me. And if I choose to speak your language, that implies it is 'better' than mine. All cultures resist this kind of subordination.

Furthermore, from a more abstract and philosophical point

of view, it is possible to argue that the dominance of any language/culture/world-view is a bad thing, and that the dominance of the English/male/European/scientific perspective in particular is a bad thing. Those who raise these criticisms of a world language insist that technocratic society diminishes important human values, and that European cultural imperialism is prejudiced and inhumane in its treatment of various groups.

Certainly there is some truth in both of these arguments. To date, cultural dominance has been in large part driven by imperialistic values that most right-thinking people (including me) reject, and much of it has been imposed by military force and economic exploitation of the most reprehensible kind. Yet this is not the whole story.

The two dominant sources of our (Euro-American) cultural heritage are the ideas passed down from ancient Greece and Rome and the Judeo-Christian tradition. It is instructive to note that the Greeks conquered very little of the world and the Jews almost none. Their ideas, it is true, have been *spread* by the military, economic, and cultural imperialisms of others, but this was almost never done in the languages or by the people who created them. Ideas, it seems, have a force of their own, and most of the best ideas can be translated to some degree into any language, including a world language. Indeed, one could argue that the two principal examples of semi-universal languages in the past, church Latin and Diplomatic French, were made possible and desirable by central ideas derived from other cultures.

At any rate, it seems clear that the elimination of classical Greek and ancient Hebrew as living languages did not destroy all the important ideas from those cultures. But perhaps the death of these languages contributed to the decline of the cultures from which they sprang. Is this a bad thing, and should we try to avoid it in the future?

The 'politically correct' view of the moment is that we need to preserve our cultural heritages in all their glorious diversity and that anything that threatens a currently existing way of life is *ipso facto* a bad thing.

With some trepidation, I disagree.

It is true that all cultures deserve the right of self-determination. It is also true that it is generally a good thing for people to be proud of their culture and their ancestors and to understand and accept their own origins. It does not follow from these facts that we should preserve all cultures from change, even if that were possible.

Interestingly enough, one of the most forthright assertions that it *does* follow that we should preserve existing cultures occurs in the (technocratic) science fiction series *Star Trek* and *Star Trek – The Next Generation*, where the 'Prime Directive' governing the crew of the starship *Enterprise* in their explorations of the universe is never to interfere in the development of any local culture. (The philosophical force of this attitude is perhaps somewhat obviated by the artistic device of pretending that most cultures speak English, so that snappy dialogue does not have to pass interminably through the universal translator.)

For galactic explorers, it no doubt makes sense to avoid meddling on first contact with alien beings. Within our own family, however, meddling is something that we do (and should do) best.

The entire issue of culture change is complicated and fraught with philosophical difficulties. Perhaps I should admit straightaway that my own viewpoint is only partly rational and is partly the result of personal experience – I am the product of a dying culture and damned glad to leave it behind.

When I was born, my family lived in a log cabin in the hills of Arkansas. We had no electricity and no indoor plumbing. My father plowed with a team of horses and my mother hauled water to the cookstove for our baths. What may seem to condescending liberals to be an idyllic, pastoral existence seemed to us to be a hard row to hoe, and none of us would go back to it. (As you might expect, I resonate to the words of the song: 'The summer folk call it Paradise Mountain, but we call it Poverty Hill.'[2])

Most of that culture is dying now. Some of its best and worst aspects survive – my mother still prefers to live in a small, friendly town, and some of my childhood friends are still racists. Despite these links to the dying culture, however, none of them would give up their automobiles, tractors, running water, and television sets. They thank (or should thank) Franklin Roosevelt, the federal government, and the Rural Electrification Act for helping them to escape what Marx called 'the idiocy of rural life,'[3] and they have mostly come to see that the world is changing and that bigotry and ignorance should be conquered rather than embraced. The point of this personal aside is that in many – perhaps most – cases, even the 'victims' of culture change will agree that it was, on balance, a good thing. To prevent them from having the opportunity to make the change is condescension and paternalism of the worst sort.

I conclude, then, that we should not generally force other cultures to change (although for unhappy, exploitative, or slave-owning societies even that is debatable), but neither should we fear change as such or preserve what exists merely because it exists. When we changed from tribalists to nationalists we lost one identity and adopted another. When we become internationalists we change again. In both cases, it seems to me, the changes are for the better and should not be artificially impeded.

The inevitability of a world language

Arguments concerning the morality and desirability of establishing a world language are important and instructive. Nevertheless, at the risk of sounding vaguely Marxist, I want to argue that for economic and cultural reasons, the development of a world language is *inevitable*. It is inevitable as the creation of worldwide mathematical and musical languages was inevitable, and as the eventual worldwide spread of the metric system of measurement is inevitable, despite the USA's idiotic resistance.

In the case of music and mathematics, anyone can see that we are all better off if thinkers around the world share a common means for distributing and evaluating their work as directly and understandably as possible. In the case of the metric system, the inherent rationality and ease of use of a decimal system of measurement is a major factor, and the economic advantage of standardization provides the market force for its dissemination. I know of no one who seriously argues that the old foot-pound system currently employed in the United States is intrinsically or intellectually *better* than the metric system. The *only* arguments – and they have thus far prevailed – against adoption of the metric system in my country are the *very same kind* of argument as those raised against a world language: cultural inertia, ethnocentrism, self-interest, and an emphasis on 'preserving' the past. Why should these arguments seem so obviously shallow and unimportant in this context (to most thinking people), yet generate such powerful appeal when applied to language in general (to many of those same thinking people)?

The metric system is becoming – and will become – the world language of measurement. It is rapidly being assimilated into the everyday culture of most countries, but it got to this point as the language of science and commerce. In a similar fashion, as we enter the twenty-first century, English is becoming the *de facto* world language, and its spread and eventual universal adoption will follow the pattern of the symbolisms of mathematics, music, and measurement. Already English is the most popular *second* language in the world.

My two European trips, separated by sixteen years, dramatically demonstrated this point to me. Whereas in 1972 it was unusual to find everyday people who spoke English, by 1988 it was unusual to be in a situation where there was not at least someone who did.

Over the course of my recent European sabbatical, my family traveled in fourteen different countries that were home to roughly ten different languages. It would not have been practical to learn all the languages needed to get around in those countries if there were no world language. To treat all languages equally around the world in the coming era of frequent travel and worldwide commerce would require each of us to be not merely bilingual but multilingual, *extremely* multilingual. While the study of foreign languages may indeed be intrinsically desirable, it is not *that* desirable.

The collective rationality of humanity has recognized the importance of a world language, and is about the business of constructing one. This fact is perhaps not obvious if we merely look at language statistics.

A first glance shows that the greatest number of users of a single language is the 864 million speakers of Mandarin.[4] Furthermore, from 1985 to 1991, the number of Mandarin speakers increased by 109 million – by far the largest absolute increase. But if we are looking at trends, no doubt we will be more impressed with the fact that Hindi increased by 28 percent during this period (while the world population increased only 12 percent). Yet, of the twelve major languages with more than 100 million users, the language that increased the most as a percentage of world citizens is Arabic, which increased its 'market share' from 3 to 3.7 percent, for a 23 percent growth in its percentage of world citizens.

In general, the fastest-growing linguistic communities are the relatively localized Third World languages. Most European languages are actually declining as a percentage of world language users, with the exception of Spanish and (barely) Portuguese, both of which benefit from the high birth rate in their largely Catholic former colonies.

It might seem, then, to one who studies numerical trends, that the world is heading towards increased linguistic fragmentation and, barring that, if you have to bet on a world language you should bet on Mandarin, Hindi, Arabic, or Spanish.

I believe, of course, that despite these numerical trends we are in fact well on our way towards developing a world language, and that language will be English. First let me give some anecdotal evidence, then some arguments.

Anecdotal evidence 1: incident at the French inn

During my recent European sabbatical my family and I stopped for dinner in a middle-sized French town. Our halting French and our waiter's somewhat better English got us through the practical task of ordering a meal. It was markedly easier to order meals on this trip than before, but the striking thing in this case was the conversation at the next table. A French businessman was entertaining two Japanese visitors and they were speaking English. It would not have been very surprising if the Japanese had been speaking French. It would have been very unusual if the Frenchman had been speaking Japanese. It was understandable that they settled on English, which each of them had independent reasons to learn. *It would have been astonishing if they had used any other language*. It is a fact that if you choose three countries at random, you are more likely to get by in English than in any other language chosen independently. Business people are becoming aware of this, so business people are learning English and, more importantly, encouraging their schools to teach it as part of the standard preparation of future employees.

Anecdotal evidence 2: the professors' world congress

As I mentioned in Chapter 3, part-way through my family's most recent European trip I had the opportunity to participate in a world congress of organizations of professors. The meeting was held in Oslo, and there were around fifteen countries participating. Only about three of these countries had English as a native language, and England did not even participate, but the proceedings were conducted *entirely in English*. A couple of years later, the group was expanded to admit members from Eastern and Southern Europe, but the rules continued to specify that all business must be conducted in English and no delegate would be seated who did not speak English. The reasons, which proved sufficient for these highly rational individuals, were: (a) universal translation is an enormously complex, inefficient, and expensive way to conduct the business of an organization; (b) selecting a few 'official' languages only partly reduces the cost, while introducing the difficult political question of which languages are 'major'; therefore (c) the conference should use only one language, and (d) since English is now *the* international language, it follows that (e) the conference should be conducted entirely in English. (The United States does not dominate this group and did not even participate when the rules were originally adopted – the main historical influence came from the Scandinavian countries where English is already well on the way to becoming a *universal* second language.)

What both of these stories indicate, I believe, is that we are creating a world language, generally from the top down, for purposes of trade, diplomatic, and intellectual exchange. 'For several years now English has been accepted in virtually every part of the world as the preferred second language – the language that two people will turn to when they cannot understand each other's tongue.'[5] Those non-Mandarin-speakers who have a specific personal interest in China may indeed learn Mandarin as a second language. Many English-speakers will continue to learn French, German, or Spanish as a second language. But by and large and on the whole, if you had to counsel a person chosen at random from the world population about the usefulness of learning a second language, the rational answers would be (a) yes, you should learn a second language, for intellectual, cultural, and economic reasons, and (b) that language should be English.

English is currently the second most widely spoken language in the world. As of 1991, the ranking of the twelve languages with more than 100 million speakers was: Mandarin (864 million speakers in 1991), English (443), Hindi (352), Spanish (341), Russian (293), Arabic (197), Bengali (184),

Portuguese (173), Malay-Indonesian (142), Japanese (125), French (121), and German (118).

Now Mandarin is almost entirely a localized language. The Chinese culture is not imperialistic and, for now at least, is neither economically nor intellectually so successful that it inspires many admirers. Since the Chinese government is attempting to curb the growth of population, we can expect that Mandarin will level out as a proportion of world language speakers in nearly perfect correlation with the population of China as a percentage of world population.

Hindi and Bengali are in roughly the same situation as Mandarin, except that India and Pakistan have made far less inroads on population growth. These two may continue to climb in the language ratings as their populations grow, but they seem to have no taste or prospects for expanding into the world community.

Spanish is, to my mind, the only credible alternative to English as a world language. It is not confined to one nation, nor even to one continent, but is used in many countries. As a romance language, it is intrinsically easy to learn and linguistically similar to other descendants of Latin. And, with their historical ties to Catholicism, Spanish-speaking countries will probably be among the last to adopt reasonable population control measures and will reproduce more prolifically than most for the next century or so. I therefore expect Spanish to continue to expand its 'installed base' to the point where it may even briefly challenge English for the number two spot in the numerical rankings. But in the long run, the cultural, technological, intellectual and entertainment advantages of English will outdo Spanish. Already far more native speakers of Spanish are finding it useful to learn English than the other way around. Such trends will continue and reinforce each other until the growth of English as a second language completely overwhelms the growth of Spanish as a first language.

Russian had a run at becoming the world language, as Marxism/Leninism had a run at becoming the world ideology.

The two are now declining together. Indeed, as the Union of Soviet Socialist Republics disappears into history, enough of the formerly member nations may reject Russian linguistic domination to bring about an actual decrease in the number of Russian speakers (though I view this as unlikely). More to the point, as the former member nations enter the world community as independent states, they will find it increasingly important for their leadership and economic communities to acquire English, and their children will discover television and rock 'n' roll. I predict that English will displace Russian as the leading second language in most of these countries in less than a century, possibly less than a decade.

Arabic is perhaps the most troubling challenger to English as a world language, because if it should come to dominate the world, the world would have to change more radically than for any of the other contenders. Of course it is not Arabic itself that occasions these concerns, but its most significant means of expansion – the Islamic religion. Just as the growth of Spanish is largely a function of the Roman Catholic Church's expansionism and rejection of birth control, so too is the expansion of Arabic primarily a function of the spread of Islam and the growth of population in Islamic countries.

Now the spread of Islam by force is, I believe, essentially a thing of the past, in part because of the maturity and reduced aggressiveness of the religion and its leaders, but primarily because the rest of the world community is about to put a stop to all wars of aggression, including religious crusades. Furthermore, I believe the features of Islamic society that are most foreign to Euro/Americans are primarily the artifacts of poverty and ignorance rather than the language and religion. Thus, if Islam/Arabic should find the means to conquer the world, it would probably also acquire the tolerant cosmopolitanism that goes with travel and wealth, and would adapt in many ways to the subjugated countries.

But, ultimately, I believe that the close connection between Arabic and Islam, like the close connection between Mandarin and China, precludes any real possibility that Arabic will become the world language unless Islam becomes the world religion, and the time for that is past.

Portuguese has the same problems as Spanish, and Malay-Indonesian has the same problems as Hindi and Bengali – except even more so in each case – so they are scarcely credible at all as candidates for the world language.

Japan's economic power may yet increase the spread of its language, but during the period 1985–91 the relative stability of its population and the general absence of military or cultural imperialism caused its market share to decline by 8 percent. Furthermore, the rate at which the Japanese are acquiring English is far greater than the rate at which other cultures pursue Japanese. Hence, those few non-Japanese who have been making the effort to learn Japanese will soon find that English will serve those needs just as well and have many more uses besides, so there will be fewer and fewer outside speakers of Japanese rather than more and more.

The remaining major languages of the world, French and German, are actually going to be the first to decline. In both cases, national populations are fairly stable, while colonialism is a thing of the past, so the population of native speakers is scarcely growing at all. French – largely because of population growth in former French colonies – fell only slightly behind the growth of world population. German grew hardly at all and saw its percentage of world language users diminish from 2.5 to 2.2 percent, for an actual 12 percent decline of market share, the greatest among the major languages. In both cases, I believe, the same forces are at work.

First, both France and Germany have played major roles in the development of world culture and world science. In the nineteenth century, all educated people learned French. A colleague of mine recalls that in the early part of this century, 'We all had to learn German because German was the language of science.'[6] This cultural dominance is behind us now and, if I am right, no nation will ever again dominate world culture or, if it does, it will have to do it in the world language (which will be English and its descendants).

Furthermore, both France and Germany had a run at world domination through force and, while the memories of Hitler are fresher than those of Napoleon, many nations of the world remember both of these countries as aggressive in ways that, by and large, English-speaking nations have not been.

For years, now, French and German have dominated the second-language market. In Europe, it was important to master these languages for the sake of commerce. In Great Britain and the United States they were the natural choices for those with no special need for Latin, say, or Spanish. In other countries, the chance that a tourist or visiting business person would speak either French or German was, for a time, greater than the chance that he or she would speak English.

But now English is becoming the second language of choice on the continent. And even the highly multilingual Europeans have some limit to their accomplishments, so, as English is added to their lists, something else slips off. As English gets added to *everybody's* list, the need for other languages declines (since the citizens of each country will now be able to speak English). And so we are facing the probability that French and German, given their somewhat artificial prominence, will be among the first of the major languages to decline. Neither will disappear for quite some time – minor languages and languages of underdeveloped countries will be the first to go. Indeed, French and German will probably linger on longer than most other languages, because of the rich cultural heritage and national tradition of each. But in the short run, they have the most to lose as English rises.

Two current events illustrate the rapid progress of this trend to using English everywhere. In 1992 the government of the Netherlands eliminated the requirement that post-secondary education must be conducted in Dutch. Some universities indicated they would immediately begin a gradual switch to English.

Most striking of all is the dominance of English in the proceedings of the European Community. Brussels, which aspires to be the capital of Europe, has adopted English as its lingua franca. If the business of Europe is to be conducted in English, and the business of the United States is conducted in English, then the business of the world will be conducted in English. The language of world trade and government will, in the end, become the world language, and one of the ancient dividers of humanity (think of the significance of the Tower of Babel) will finally be eliminated.

Finally, let me say that the whole debate about the desirability of a world language is rapidly being deprived of practical significance by events. As I was researching this book, one of my most up-to-date sources was the electronic version of the *Academic American Encyclopedia*, available on-line on the Prodigy computer network. In that continuously updated and very *au courant* reference work, David Yerkes had written in his article on 'the English Language':

> English has a larger vocabulary than any other language; and *because it is the world language*, words newly coined or in vogue in one language are very often added to English as well.[7]

World music

In ordinary language, when we speak of the 'culture' of an area, one of the things high on our list of ingredients is the music of the area. More than any other time in history, the music people around the world listen to is now the same music.

Anecdotal evidence 3: the incident of 'real Dutch music'

While you might reasonably suspect otherwise from the tenor of my argument, my family and I very much respect the traditions and cultures of other countries and enjoy learning about them. During our stay in Amsterdam, we made a point of going out for *rijstaffel*, the marvelously varied 'rice table' cuisine that the Dutch brought home from Indonesia. We fell into conversation with some local patrons, one of whom invited us to take a ride on his canal boat. Since we try to be both trusting and adventurous, we accepted. As we headed off down the canal, we were even more pleased when he suggested that we motor over to a local festival where we would hear some 'real Dutch music.'

At the festival we found that the music was in fact a karaoke-style sing-along, where various performers would bring up a cassette tape of instrumental accompaniment and sing with a live microphone. They sang primarily in English, and we already knew many of the songs. Three times we heard the 1950s American hit 'You'll never walk alone,' which at that time was enjoying a revival throughout Europe. We never heard any music that struck *us* as Dutch, although our Dutch companions viewed it as theirs.

Music, indeed, is another one of the forces uniting us into a world community. The most striking current phenomenon is 'That damned rock music is everywhere,' and indeed it is. The rock culture of our youth is becoming strongly trans-national, and English is its dominant language. The musical tradition that grew out of American jazz, country music, and blues has incorporated variously the Indian sitar and Jamaican reggae and now sounds as natural to an Indonesian teenager as to a German youth. *They* make no fuss over the national or cultural background of their stars – they care only about the quality of the music.

Even earlier, the tradition of Western classical music began to be a major part of a world culture and a unifying force in world civilization. The other night I had an epiphany of sorts when, as I was having my nightcap, it struck me that I was drinking French wine while reading Rousseau (in English trans-lation, to be sure). Reflecting on how the noble savages would probably prefer, if given the choice, to be part of the French culture rather than their own, so that they too could enjoy Rousseau and Chablis, I realized that *I* had not chosen to be 'in the French culture' as such, but was still enjoying its fruits. And in addition to those pleasures, I happened to be listening to a compact disk recording (Dutch technology, played on a Japanese compact disk player through a German amplifier and American speakers) of a Chinese conductor leading a Hungarian orchestra in a performance of a Beethoven (Austrian) symphony. Furthermore, the clothes I was wearing had come from Korea, Mexico, and France, and my wine glass from Denmark. My little moment of relaxation was *already* part of a world culture, and Western classical music has been a major component of that culture for generations.

International television

Just as Western classical music became international during the last two centuries, and rock 'n roll spread around the globe during this century, international television will be a major force uniting the world of the twenty-first century.

Television is the most accessible medium for most people. It is increasingly available, and increasingly popular. TV programs cross national borders both directly, as broadcasts (so that many Estonians, for example, watch Finnish television) and indirectly, by distribution through international markets. Soon television will be even more universally available and homogeneous, as direct broadcast satellites begin beaming directly from space to receivers across the globe. Finally, the universal spread of video cassette recorders (some 62 percent of US households had VCRs in 1990) multiplies both the accessibility and the universality of television programming.

In addition to its widespread availability, television programming is highly accessible conceptually. It provides a strong visual content, and its audio track can be either dubbed into a different language or supplemented with subtitles. In the first system, the content passes across linguistic barriers; in the second, it experiences a symbiotic growth with world English, as people learn the second language through hearing English and reading the subtitles. Either way, the growth of international television will inevitably help to create a world culture.

Already most of the political leaders we see on the nightly television news programs have adopted the standard business suit – this is the way you dress in today's world if you want to be respected, and, except for ceremonial and nationalistic occasions, it is substantially the same the world over.

And the movies or situation comedies that follow the news are far more likely to be originally produced in English than in any other language. If you want to be successful as a 'world-class' star at almost anything, you need to learn English in order to deal with the entertainment 'industry.'

The hypothetical extra-terrestrial intelligence

One final, more speculative, force I see contributing to the conceptual development of a world culture. The hypothetical extra-terrestrial intelligence that was once the conjecture of science-fiction 'fanatics' is now receiving sober consideration. The search for extra-terrestrial intelligence has received funding from several governments, and the project is engaged in sampling the electromagnetic spectrum for messages from the stars.

At the same time, we are sending messages out to other solar systems. Some of these are consciously designed, such as the plaques on Pioneer 10 and 11 and the recordings on Voyagers 1 and 2, intended to be self-translating messages to any sentient beings who might discover them. Others, though, are inadvertent by-products of civilization, such as the expanding globe of modulated radio and television signals that has already passed the nearest stars and continues to diffuse through the universe.

The possibility that some contact will eventually be made with other sentient beings is growing in popular acceptance. Some of this is based on monster movies and the fringe UFO (unidentified flying object) movement. But some of it is also reasonable speculation, based in part upon a growing awareness of the size of the universe, in part upon the declining belief in geocentric religions, and in part upon the scientific evidence that we are not so incomprehensibly complex as to require miraculous creation, so our analogues might easily spring up elsewhere.

Some good science fiction stories have suggested that if and when we *do* encounter an alien civilization, it will forcibly create an awareness of our own civilization as an organic whole, contrasted starkly against the *non*-human culture of the others. But my claim that cultural interdependence is fostered by alien civilizations does not require that such civilizations actually exist, or that we encounter them any time soon. It is sufficient that millions of people are facing the *possibility* that they might exist, and are learning to think of our world, in contrast, as a human world, rather than a British island or French province. As we conceptually sketch in the contrast that might exist, we become more aware of the unity that does exist.

The USA as world culture

Finally, let me face up to the problem that the world culture, as I anticipate its development, will be substantially an American culture.

There are two great complaints frequently raised against US culture: (a) Americans have no culture, and (b) Americans are arrogant about their non-existent culture. For example, Americans often make the following kinds of boast:

1. We were right about democracy.
2. We were right about capitalism.
3. We were right about the English language.
4. We won all the wars.
5. We invented rock music.
6. Hollywood, Wall Street, and Madison Avenue are American places and world institutions.
7. We refuse to learn any other languages.
8. We think of ourselves as policemen of the world.

The explanation for much of the character and much of the

dominance of American culture is this: American culture is entirely eclectic and substantially derivative.

Native Americans play almost no role in American culture. America is a nation of immigrants, and a new nation at that. Most of its best ideas came from elsewhere: the English created the language; the Greeks invented democracy; the Dutch brought capitalism to the new world; Jewish immigrants played key roles in Hollywood, Wall Street, and Madison Avenue; German scientists built America's nuclear bombs and rockets; American cuisine comes from everywhere; and even the Beatles were British!

The coming world culture will indeed be like the American culture – it will be like it in a universal willingness to consider ideas from any source, to find beauty in many traditions, and to accept people from any background as free and equal citizens. Much that we think of as characteristically American will become characteristically human, much will disappear, and some will remain as a regional variation in the world culture. (Even if western US citizens eventually speak the same language and drive the same cars as the Japanese, for example, proportionately more Texans than Japanese will probably still ride horses and raise cattle.)

Those who believe deeply in cultural diversity are doing the rest of us a favor by helping to preserve some of the immense variety of the human experience, just as the environmentalists are doing us a favor by helping to preserve the variety of living species on the globe. The danger is that it is not possible to preserve a living culture – cultures change of necessity, and the rate of cultural change is rapidly accelerating. When we actively seek to preserve a way of life, then, we can do so only by trapping some people in the past (as we have to trap some animals in zoos). Left to themselves, both animals and cultures evolve. The only way to *prevent* the development of a world culture is to *forbid* some human societies to change. We should not do that if we could.

It does no good to wring one's hands about the loss of the past. We can treasure our childhood memories and cling to mementos of the past, but we can't stay in kindergarten forever.[8] The human race – to survive at all, much less to flourish – needs to become one family. As we move towards that goal, it will be impossible to prevent or avoid the development of a world culture. Those who value cultural alternatives will have to find other ways to preserve them. Tribalism is behind us forever, and nationalism is on the way out. The worst fears of patriots and jingoists everywhere are about to be realized: we are finally about to become One World, One Government, One Culture.

9 Environmental interdependence

It is a commonplace that growing environmental awareness and beautiful pictures of our planet taken from space are causing more and more people to try to preserve their little part of the environment.

This effort is wonderful and can even be decisive for cases such as toxic waste and water pollution, where the source and the effects are generally confined to the same country. But some types of environmental concerns are starting to put a strain on our traditional system of independent, sovereign, nation-states. It may no longer be enough to 'think globally, act locally.' The solution to some of our problems will require us to act globally as well – something we are not at present equipped to do.

Acid rain

Acid rain is this type of environmental problem. In this case, the polluting effects may well be across a national boundary from the pollution emitters. What recourse, then, does the sufferer have? Can Switzerland sue the industrial plants in northern Italy? Should Canada bomb the United States? In the absence of a world government, there is no institution presently capable of enforcing pollution control around the globe. Still, acid rain is one of the more tractable international problems. It, at least, almost always originates in a developed country with cultural and economic ties to the countries it is harming. In such a situation, diplomacy and political pressure may well cause the offending nation to mend its ways.

The destruction of the rain forest

A more telling case is that of the destruction of the world's rain forests. Typically, this occurs in underdeveloped nations as a means of attaining the economic wealth we have taught them to desire. And the harm involved is not direct, observable, and focussed on one or a few other nations.

The most commonly cited undesirable effects of deforestation are the extinction of species and the reduction of the world's ability to generate oxygen for the atmosphere. These are both somewhat abstract and, to an extent, debatable. In the case of oxygen depletion, for example, it is perfectly possible for the offenders to argue that the natural balance of the ecosphere will always be maintained one way or another – either by an increase of other oxygen-producing species or a decrease of oxygen-consuming species – and who is to say that one balance of species is *a priori* more desirable than another?

In the case of species loss, we run directly into one of the problems of national sovereignty. The Brazilians, for example, quite reasonably maintain that the plants and animals in their national boundary are *their* natural resources and if they choose to destroy them, or use them for economic growth, *it is nobody else's business*. This response is both natural and morally justified if we accept the presumption that individualistic capitalism is the proper moral model for international relations. After all, who has the *right* to tell Brazil what it may do with its own property?

Most advanced nations have accepted the internal principle that individual property rights must sometimes yield to the common good. Zoning laws, tree ordinances, endangered species acts and so on are democratically imposed restrictions on the right of the individual to engage in socially harmful behavior *even if* it involves only wholly owned personal property. Such laws force all individuals to surrender rights that had previously been held to be 'natural.' As Eric T. Freyfogle put it, 'so long as private ownership means the right to use, alter and destroy at will, national environmental health can be little more than a dream.'[1]

In the case of international relations, however, few have drawn the analogous conclusion that world environmental health can be little more than a dream so long as national sovereignty means 'the right to use, alter and destroy at will.' Furthermore, even if enlightened environmentalists do reach this conclusion, there is no forum for them to address these issues, because no democratic government exists that has the right and the authority to demand that a nation stop engaging in such behavior. And it would be arrant paternalism of the worst kind for developed nations to use their economic or military might to force underdeveloped countries to conform to externally imposed standards while they themselves refuse to do so.

Yet, if we have the right to enforce any environmental laws at all, surely we should have the right to enforce those against international ecological mischief because, as Henry Shue says, 'While harming oneself may sometimes be immoral, it is harming others that ought generally to be illegal.'[2]

It may be that the morally important change in our world is a result of our newly developed ability to affect each other's lives over great distances. Judith Lichtenberg has suggested that today's world is both practically and morally different from the world of our ancestors:

> Though we have excellent reason to believe that life, even intelligent life, exists in other parts of the universe, at this time we seem to have no reasons to think that the behavior of earthlings impinges on such life or does so in a significant way. Certainly we do not know *how* our actions do or could affect life in other parts of the universe. So our world at this time does not extend beyond the boundaries of the

planet. It seems extremely plausible that, at this stage of human history, *the limits of the planet are the limits of our world.* It also seems plausible that this was not always so: that there used to be more and smaller worlds. If true, these facts would explain much not only about individuals' and groups' obligations but also about their beliefs about their obligations.

What constitutes a world today? What constituted a world yesterday? Do these differ? These are empirical questions. The answers depend on which individuals, groups, or societies do impinge on each other, and which can.[3]

Whatever might have been the appropriate level of environmental regulation for the world of our ancestors, it is clear that now we need to develop a concept of world resources and a government to regulate those resources. There must be worldwide endangered species laws, and only a world legislature can promulgate such laws. There must be international inspection and enforcement of these laws, and only a world executive can do this. There must be just compensation for those who bear the economic burden of protecting the environment, and only a world court can accomplish this, with funds raised through a system of world taxation.

The dangers of ethical imperialism

The concept of world resources is an essential one; it is also, however, a dangerous one.

As has been demonstrated in many cases of imperialistic exploitation, the developed nations' concept of sharing has all too often been 'what's yours is mine, and what's mine is mine.' Typically it has been seen as the 'duty' of underdeveloped nations to provide their natural resources (and their cheap labor) to meet the needs of industries from which they did not benefit.

Whenever a war threatens in the Middle East, or some government or cartel restricts the production of oil, there are always voices heard to proclaim: 'they have no right to deny us the oil that we need.' Sometimes this claim is supported by a reasonable view of the collective ownership of natural resources, but this is rare. The usual case is a blatant claim that such 'two-bit countries' have no right to frustrate the desires of the industrialized nations *because* they are rich and powerful and accustomed to getting their way.

It would grieve me deeply if my notion of world resources came to be used as a justification by rapacious jingoists.

If human society becomes more like a family, it is true that we will be less and less inclined to allow one person or group of persons to assert exclusive ownership of anything that is needed by all. Not that private property is inconsistent with familial ties – I believe we will always have special attachments to some valued items of personal ownership. But the notion that one person should 'own' vast stretches of land or huge deposits of oil will someday seem as outdated and incomprehensible as the belief that one person should 'own' other people. To this extent, the jingoists' cry is true – they don't have 'the right' to deny us 'their' oil.

But neither do we have the contrary right to take their oil without compensation. As we move from one value system and social order to another, we must be careful not to spread the benefits and the sacrifices unfairly. No doubt there must be a significant redistribution of wealth within – and especially among – the existing nations. No accidents of history or just compensation for personal efforts could possibly justify a world that allows millions of children to starve, millions of others to face a life with no home, no job, and no hope for the future.

This seems to me to be so clear and incontestable that I am inclined to say, in the spirit of the Harvard Paradigm, that if a moral theory sanctions injustice on such a vast scale, it is probably a theory that needs to be revised. The Harvard Paradigm is a meta-philosophical conception of the relationship between theory and evidence. It was developed at Harvard and manifests itself in the epistemology of Willard van

Orman Quine and Nelson Goodman, the mathematical views of Hilary Putnam, the philosophy of science of Thomas Kuhn, and the ethical theory of John Rawls.

The fundamental principle of the Harvard Paradigm is essentially pragmatic and can be expressed in the following two theses: (1) There are no *a priori* truths or other epistemologically basic propositions, and (2) The interplay of theory and evidence is not formalizable; sometimes we adjust one, sometimes the other; and these adjustments are 'where rational, pragmatic.'[4]

The possibility that moral theories may sometimes require revision on the basis of empirical fact is one of the more important systematic contributions of the Harvard Paradigm in meta-philosophy. In this case it seems clear to me that any theory that fails to require a redistribution of the world's wealth is in need of such revision.

That a redistribution is morally justified, however, does not mean it can be undertaken or enforced by the aggrieved party or any other non-institutionalized group that merely seeks to 'do what's right.'

Let us assume, for example, that the United States' attack on Iraq was both morally justified and sanctioned by the United Nations' resolutions on the matter. The US invasions of Grenada and Panama were (we will further assume for the sake of discussion) morally justified but not sanctioned by international authority. On these assumptions, is it not intuitively obvious that the US has a *better claim* to be justified in its actions in the first case than in the latter two?

Similarly, if Great Britain should decide to force Brazil to stop cutting down its rain forests, Britain would be doing what is right, but would not have the right to do it.

Interference of one nation in the affairs of another is justifiable only if (1) there is a supranational authority to justify it, or (2) nations are not moral entities.

There is indeed an inconsistency between the notion of global resources and the concept of absolute national sovereignty. I believe that the environmental interdependence of the world will inevitably resolve that conflict in favor of the notion of global resources. National sovereignty must therefore yield in this matter – but yield to what?

One possibility is to have the United States and other gunslinging do-gooder countries going around the world, forcing nations to behave. In many cases this would work – in most it would not. Overwhelming military force remains a very blunt instrument, even in the era of 'smart bombs.' It is ill suited to enforce the many sophisticated distinctions that will be required by our increasing ecological and economic interdependence.

Much work has already been done on issues of this sort by various international commissions, UN agencies, and voluntary treaty groups. I do not mean to derogate that work – it has played a valuable role in making international cooperation familiar and respectable, in addition to the immediate good it has accomplished.

But the world's problems cannot be solved by voluntary international cooperation, any more than a city's problems can be solved by charitable contributions. I believe, in fact, that the attempt to solve social problems by voluntary cooperation and individual charity is not just impractical, it is socially pernicious and ethically unjustified!

The effect of relying on voluntary efforts is this: the good people of the society make their contribution, and thus become worse off; the bad people of the society do not make a contribution and thus become (at least relatively) better off. Any scheme that systematically advantages bad people at the expense of good people is *ipso facto* wrong. Therefore reliance on individual charity to solve social problems is ethically wrong.

The only (or at least, the only obviously) fair way to solve a social problem is to agree democratically on what the problem is and how to solve it, and to use taxation to spread the cost fairly through the population. This implies that when problems are international, their solution will require the existence of a supranational government capable of making and enforcing decisions, and capable of taxing its members to finance its actions. Our global environmental interdependence therefore poses a very strong argument for an effective world government.

It may also have a profound effect on the future of religion and the family. The Catholic thinkers Sally and Philip Scharper have gone so far as to argue that

> The Church will eventually realize that there is a theological dimension to ecology, and will revive its ancient, but long-forgotten understanding that man is not the master of creation, but steward over it. The ruthless exploitation of the earth and ocean (which usually involves the exploitation of other human beings) will be seen as sinful, since it violates man's primal mandate to enter into creative partnership with nature.
>
> From this theological position the Church will move next to the realization that she is the guardian of the quality of life – a role the Church had assumed in its sponsoring of schools, its preservation of the classics of antiquity, its protection of serf and peasant, its elevation of woman (despite the myopia of some of her great theologians), her efforts to impose peace or at least 'humanize' the conduct of warfare.
>
> In the context of the ecological crisis the Church might well exhort the married to limit the number of their children to one or two, a sacrifice to be made in the interests of 'the greater good,' a concept that has long been a hinge-concept in scholastic philosophy and Catholic moral theology.
>
> For those capable of 'a yet more excellent way,' the Church may recommend having no children, for theological reasons not too dissimilar from those long advanced to support priestly celibacy and the religious vow of chastity.
>
> We may, then, in the foreseeable future see one of those ironies with which 'God is so prodigal,' in the words of Paul Claudel. The Church, within a generation, may be

suggesting though press and pulpit that those couples who refuse to limit their families are guilty of selfishness – a charge leveled by the Church for years against those who did limit their families through means of artificial contraception.[5]

10 What is important?

Thus far I have dealt with the problems of world peace and the human family primarily from an institutional point of view. I have argued that we must reconstitute world society in order to avoid the horror of war and in order to improve the lot of world citizens.

I believe that such an institutional approach is justified by the moral attitudes of the ordinary person, but it is not, perhaps, obviously so. Part of the reason is that the moral attitudes of ordinary persons are seldom ordered by systematic moral theories, and part of the problem is that these theories, when they do exist, are often wrong.

To create a world society of peace, justice, and freedom, it is important to show that such a society follows naturally from the best moral theory. We must have a moral theory that is philosophically sound, personally attractive, and practically workable. It must be acceptable to human beings as they are, while guiding them to what they ought to become. Above all, it must be based on a realistic view of human behavior.

The relationship between human behavior, moral systems, and social institutions is a complex one. I believe that the core of this relationship is best described by the philosophical position that I call 'The Harvard Paradigm,' which says that in some cases we adjust our theories to fit the evidence, but in some other cases we modify the evidence to fit the theory.

We would naturally like to believe that our institutions are guided by our ethical beliefs. To some extent, this is so, but in many ways it manifestly is not. The obvious first impediment is that there is no such thing as 'our ethical beliefs' – in a culturally diverse society we find a multiplicity of beliefs, some of which are systematic, most of which are not, and many of which are in conflict.

The second problem is that the relation between our moral beliefs and our institutions is not unidirectional. We are just as likely to alter our moral beliefs because of our institutions as we are to reform our institutions for moral reasons. Many people, for example, believe that it is wrong to kill, but, faced with the behavior of their government, manage to create an exception to that commandment. Many Americans likewise believed that racial segregation carried out under the principle of 'separate but equal' was fair and moral until the US Supreme Court and the civil rights struggle challenged that belief. And many conservatives who once believed that the notion of a Social Security Trust Fund was an instrument of atheistic communism have, in the face of institutional reality, come to accept it as a normal and moral part of American life. The interplay of ethical beliefs and institutions is unending and unpredictable.

So it is contrary to the spirit of the Harvard Paradigm to think of institutions as being 'based on' moral beliefs in any foundational sense.

The third problem with the view that our institutions are shaped by our moral views, though, is the worst. It is that most of the world subscribes to moral beliefs that are either inconsistent or practically unworkable. This applies in particular to any moral theory that declares that all individuals are (or should be) of equal value to each individual. No one is capable of taking this claim seriously enough to act upon it, yet most profess to believe it.

In what follows, I seek to sketch a moral position that reduces the conceptual dissonance between our ethics and our behavior without sacrificing the moral imperative to improve the world. What is important in this process is the fundamental recognition that each of us must value every sentient being, but this value increases or diminishes along a sliding scale of social distance.

With this conceptual realignment it becomes possible to maintain national control over matters that are appropriately national interests, while giving up the myth of national sovereignty as a universal principle. It becomes possible to recognize one's obligation to aid the starving millions without giving up one's middle-class existence. It becomes possible to require the Brazilians to stop destroying the rain forest without denying their right to a decent life.

It becomes possible, in short, to create a world society of peace, justice, and freedom.

11 Who is a person?

The fundamental moral question in constructing a society and developing a moral code to govern it is deciding who is to count as a person. Indeed, Ian Vine has claimed that 'Commitment to a moral code involves affirmative recognition of one's shared humanity with those to whom it is applied.'[1]

In this chapter I wish to argue for two seemingly innocuous and uncontroversial principles that, nevertheless, are of profound importance if taken seriously. They are:

1. Every human being is a person.
2. Nations are not persons.

Taken together with the assumption that persons are the fundamental bearers of moral rights and responsibilities, these principles should suffice to eliminate war.

Every human being is a person

Most human societies have professed, and to some extent acted upon, a belief that human beings as such have a right to be treated with dignity and consideration. The problem has been that each society has tended to be ethnocentric in its conception of who counts as human. Rather than recognize everyone equally, we choose – we 'discriminate' – between those who are acceptable and those who are not. In many respects this is our most important moral decision. As Michael Walzer says,

> The primary good that we distribute to one another is membership in some human community. And what we do with regard to membership structures all other distributive choices. It determines with whom we make those choices, from whom we require obedience and collect taxes, to whom we allocate goods and services.[2]

All too often, we choose not to 'distribute' this primary good, but to hoard it amongst a few and to deny it to others.

Tribal warfare has often been justified by the belief that we are the only true 'people,' while all others are barbarians. Religious warfare has often been justified by the belief that we are the only true 'children of God,' while all others are heathen infidels. Slavery, since at least the time of Aristotle, has been justified by the belief that those who are enslaved are in some way 'inferior.' Modern imperialism has often been justified by the belief that those we exploit are 'savages.'

In most cases, the admission to full human status occurs gradually over a period of growing interaction, commerce, intermarriage, and cultural assimilation. In some cases, however, Glynis M. Breakwell has argued, fully human status is accorded to groups after we become *less* economically dependent on their exploitation. Thus the recent expansion of interest in child welfare laws and equal rights for blacks coincided with the 'decline in demand for slave labor' and the 'redundancy' of child labor.[3] In any event, there is a clear historical trend towards extending what Vine called the 'moral ingroup.' The logical, and seemingly theoretically necessary, outcome of this development is to extend membership to all human beings.

So the best of our modern moral systems have tried to combat the evils of ethnocentrism and xenophobic prejudice by asserting that all human beings are equal, that God loves us all, that color, gender, socioeconomic status, and cultural level are morally irrelevant. It follows, then, that it is our duty to care for everyone equally – to work as hard to save the starving children in Ethiopia as we would if they were our own. If our social institutions and our individual actions conformed to this moral view, the world would indeed become a better place.

Unfortunately, this is not possible.

Nobody in fact treats everyone with equal respect. We haven't the time, we haven't the resources, and we haven't the psychic energy.

The first philosophical paper I ever read to a group was entitled 'An explanation of northern inhospitality.' I presented it to the Summer Conference of Danforth Fellows in 1964. In it, I tried to explain and justify my contention that in America, small-town southerners really are friendlier than 'Yankees' (those who live in the more urbanized north). The reason I advanced is that each of us has a finite capacity for taking others seriously as persons. If we recognize every citizen of our small town, the total number of human relationships we generate remains manageably small. But, if we walk down the streets of New York City making eye contact, smiling, and saying hello to everyone, the least that will happen is that we will exhaust ourselves. As a matter of practical time management we must restrict our interest to those we 'recognize' and treat everyone else as environmental objects.

No doubt I would revise this paper, if I still had it, but the fundamental insight has been sustained and, to some extent, strengthened by subsequent observation. When I went to Harvard and actually got to know some of those big-city Yankees, I discovered that many of them were in fact friendlier and more hospitable than the small-town southerners I had known – but only if you had been 'properly introduced' and entered into the comparatively small circle they recognized as real people. By hoarding their social kindness, they became able to lavish it more generously upon smaller groups.

Whether or not these impressionistic observations are justified, it is glaringly obvious that we do not *in practice* treat all human beings as equally deserving of our time, concern, and resources. No doubt a handful of saints have sold all that they had to give to the poor, but most of us never will and can only resent being told that we 'ought to.' In practice, we do as my Yankee friends did and recognize only a small circle of family and friends as fully human.

Now to deny personhood to others is to deny that we have moral obligations to them. This process has been called 'dehumanization' and is an important step in war, exploitation, and genocide. In all too real a sense, people in the United States say that 'only' 171 died in the Gulf War. 'Enemy' fatalities are generally ignored – civilians are almost never counted. The only deaths that matter are those of 'our troops.' This horrible moral blindness is one of the most disgusting things about war – both as cause and as effect. We go to war with others in part because they are different from us, and we then magnify those differences to justify our own actions. (Even in what most Americans think of as a fully just war, World War II, they found it necessary to speak of 'the Yellow Peril' in an attempt to reassure themselves that what they were doing was right.) Clearly, much of the evil in the world is attributable to one group's dehumanization of another.

Yet it is equally clear that it is not possible for human beings to treat everyone as of equal value in practice.

In order to resolve this dilemma, and to make world peace possible, we must develop a moral theory that admits the importance of each sentient being, but apportions that importance along a sliding scale of social distance. In the next chapter I seek to develop such a system. Basically, it argues that each person is metaphysically and legally equal when viewed as the holder of natural rights and the object of negative duties (the duty not to harm thus applies equally to everyone). But all persons are not morally equal when viewed as members of *my* moral universe (or yours, or any other individual's), as the object of positive duties of benefaction (the duty to help others does *not* apply equally to all possible beneficiaries).

From the point of view of world peace, the result of thus

recognizing the influence of social distance on our moral duties is to make plausible what is otherwise incomprehensible: our willingness to let some other people starve while simultaneously claiming that we recognize moral duties to all people.

It is my hope that the modest insulating effect of social distance will finally make it possible for us to achieve the natural goal of a great historical development – the recognition of all human beings as persons.

Nations are not persons

My second modest claim about personhood is the seemingly obvious principle that nations are not persons. Oddly enough, failure to recognize this principle has caused almost as much mischief in the world as has the failure to recognize the fundamental personhood of all human beings. It has done so by the almost universal acceptance of the view that international relations are, from the moral point of view, relations between nations.

What could be more obvious than this – mere etymology should make it obvious that international relations obtain between states while intranational relations obtain within states. Yet immediately an asymmetry obtrudes: if intranational relations obtain within states, *between* what do intranational relations obtain? Clearly the usual and most important answer is, 'between persons.' And so we come quite naturally to the standard view: the moral code that obtains within national boundaries governs persons; that which obtains across national boundaries governs nations.

Two principal versions of the standard view have evolved. The *State of Nature* interpretation views nations as independent moral entities who find themselves in a world without moral principles to govern their cooperation. On the usual view, they are unable to develop such principles (unlike persons, who do develop such principles *within* nations). The second variant is the *Morality of States* view, which agrees that nations are moral entities but believes some minimal system of constraints – a sort of natural law – does apply to their interactions. Typically these rules include non-intervention and non-aggression but do not include any positive duties or enforcement devices. Nations generally are held to retain the right to make war for 'Reasons of State.'[4]

In both versions of the standard view we arrive at this conclusion: (a) international actions are the actions of nations; (b) nations have at most minimal moral obligations to each other; and (c) nations have no moral obligations at all to the citizens of other nations.

Morality between nations, then, consists almost entirely of the egoistic interaction of autonomous entities subject to no (or minimal) moral restraints. The horrors of war are justified, it seems, because they are beyond the scope of normal moral rules. Even though *I* would not have the right to bomb Baghdad, on this view, my government *does* (or, at least, might) have the right to do so, because it is subject to a different set of moral principles.

I wish to argue most strenuously against this view. I believe that the conception of nations as moral entities is the ultimate perversion of the idolatry of nationalism. The notion that thousands of real human beings can be killed in warfare and that *no one is responsible* seems to me to be about as clear a *reductio ad absurdum* of nationalistic principles as one could find.

In the world as we know it, all moral actions are the actions of individual human beings. No abstraction, collective, or community can plant a tree, feed a child, or torture a dissident. Everything that gets done is the result of one person's individual action or of two or more persons engaging in joint action for which each is responsible. Likewise every right is the right of some person and every obligation is some person's obligation. (Where we speak of groups having obligation, I maintain, they have them distributively, not collectively.) The fictional rights and obligations of corporations, for example, are actually accounting devices for fixing financial liability. The notion that a corporation is a legal person does not extend, for example, to trying a corporation for murder. But – and this is important – neither does it give a corporation the *right* to murder!

It is bad metaphysics to believe that a corporation has any actual existence over and above the existence of its owners, directors, and employees and the things they own. It is worse moral theory to believe that corporations can take action, commit crimes, or be either innocent or guilty of moral transgressions. Moral theory applies *only* to human (or other sapient) actions and it applies to *all* such actions.

In particular, no corporation has the right to kill human beings.

Now the owners, directors, or employees of a corporation *might* have a right to kill human beings. They might have it in virtue of their, so to speak, private personhood (self-defense, for example), or they might have it by virtue of office (if the security guards, after proper training and due care, are authorized to shoot to kill thieves or arsonists). But if any individual claims the right to kill by virtue of the authorization of others, then the ones who issue that authorization and the ones who act upon it continue to bear the moral responsibility for their actions and, if it turns out they *did not* have the right to issue such authorizations or commit such acts, it is they, and not the corporation, who have committed immoral acts.

I believe that nations are, from the moral point of view, just like corporations.

Nations serve as vehicles for collective actions. They provide the benefits of cooperative endeavor and efficiencies of scale to the individuals who participate in them. They require greater subordination and assert more regulative authority than do corporations, but they are – metaphysically speaking – nothing more than cooperating groups of individual human beings.

It follows from this that if *I* don't have the right to bomb Baghdad, and *you* don't have the right to bomb Baghdad, and . . . then even 250 million of us collectively would not have the right to bomb Baghdad. The rights of nations are nothing but convenient expressions of the rights of citizens. As a cooperative enterprise, we have the right to outlaw certain forms of behavior (prostitution, let us say) within our jurisdiction. We have no such right to outlaw prostitution in other areas. We certainly have no right to enforce our rules among people who do not belong to our corporation or nation. Calling ourselves a nation does not give us the right to impose our will on others.

Machiavelli claimed that the Prince was subject to different rules of morality than the rest of us.[5] The Nuremberg Trials – and most contemporary public opinion – give evidence that this was a mistake. Hitler did not have the right to invade Russia – and neither did Germany! Private individuals do not have the right to commit genocide – and neither do *Reichsmarshals*.

The belief that nations, as spiritual entities, have rights that individual humans do not is a characteristic mistake of Fascism.

War is a fundamentally Fascist institution. It depends upon and presupposes the glorification of the state, the militarization of the society, and the sacrifice of the individual. Its virtues are Fascist virtues, its defects Fascist defects. That is why there are no democratic wars of aggression, and why ultimately there must be no war.

Even in the best of wars, at least one side must be acting immorally. If the Allies were justified in resisting the Fascists, that is because the individual citizens of Germany, Japan, and Italy *did not* acquire rights of expansionism by creating 'organic' states with 'higher destinies.' This much seems settled. But what we persistently fail to realize is that the citizens of the Allied countries also *did not* acquire the right of self-defense by virtue of their citizenship. Even if Poland had been anarchic, with no government whatsoever, the Poles would still have had the right to resist the German invasion. The right of self-defense (if there is such a right) attaches to persons, not nations.

Now the counterpart of rights in moral theory is responsibilities. If I deny that nations have rights, does it not follow that I should also deny that nations have responsibilities? Yes, it does. But doesn't that imply that we cannot *punish* Iraq, say, for its illegal invasion of Kuwait? Yes, it does mean that. Punishment is a moral concept; moral concepts do not apply to nations (directly); therefore, punishment does not apply to nations.

In fact, look at what the standard view has led us to. Iraq (which we take to be a nation, a spiritual entity, a moral agent) has illegally invaded Kuwait. Therefore Iraq should be punished. Therefore we will kill tens of thousands of Iraqi soldiers. We will also (but only incidentally) kill tens of thousands of Iraqi civilians. We will make life hard 'for Iraq' by cutting off trade and embargoing all but essential supplies. That will teach Iraq a lesson!

So what have we accomplished? The individuals who physically invaded Kuwait and did reprehensible things have been injured or killed, to some extent, but there is no effective or even intended correlation between the crimes of the individual soldier and his eventual suffering at the hands of the Allies. If he got sent to the wrong place, he might be dead even if he had behaved as humanely as possible throughout; if he raped, looted, and killed, but then was reassigned to the north, no punishment ensued and he even keeps whatever loot he got away with.

The civilians have suffered considerably. No doubt they deserved to suffer a bit, since they supported or at least tolerated their government's immoral action. But again there is no clear correlation between suffering and guilt. If anything, there is likely to be a negative correlation, since those who suffer the most are generally citizens with the *least* power to make any effective difference in politics. The individuals who are really in a position to exert political power for the most part are doing just fine, thank you. The rulers, and specifically Saddam Hussein, have not suffered at all (unless you put a great deal of faith in mental anguish and loss of face).

And so the standard view comes to this: the guilt is the state's, not that of any individuals; therefore the punishment should rain at random upon the state; it would be specifically immoral to single out individuals for special pain.

Could we possibly get further from doing what is right? Perhaps, if we *intentionally* killed babies and rewarded bad men. But even this wouldn't look a whole lot different in practice from what we have in fact done. And this, you should recall, is as close to a universally sanctioned military action as the world has ever seen. Could it be that we're just going about it wrong?

What we need to do is to forget about the myth of nations as moral entities. You can't punish nations – you can only punish people. So which people deserve punishment and what is the most effective way to punish them?

To the surprise of almost everyone and the disgust of many, it turns out that, in my estimation, assassination is far preferable to warfare. Assassination – the intentional killing of specific individuals for political purposes – is universally deplored and usually outlawed. It is seldom employed by democratic governments and condemned as 'terrorism' when it is employed by others.

But if you clear away the myth of nationalism and ask, 'Who is primarily responsible for the invasion of Kuwait?' the answer is clear: Saddam Hussein and his government. So who should be punished? Those individuals. And what is the most efficient way to punish them? Kill them; or bribe someone else to kill them. But isn't killing immoral? How can the intentional, deliberate killing of a handful of miscreants be more immoral than the random destruction of thousands of innocent civilians and nearly innocent soldiers? What sort of moral sophistry can convince us that it is better to blow up factories full of workers than to stab dictators?

It might be more difficult to kill one or a few powerful individuals at a great distance than it is to mess up a city, but surely our technological efficiency and great national wealth can find a way. I'll bet the Cosa Nostra could take out a contract on Saddam Hussein for $20 million and he'd be dead by Wednesday. And if they can't do it, the CIA can. Or Mossad, if world opinion would let them. Even if it is difficult, just publishing a list of those we have found guilty and condemned to death *in absentia* might be a useful mechanism. As R. L. Holmes puts it:

> Moral considerations aside, if one's quarrel is with the leadership of a country, and one believes in the use of violence, the more rational course would be to engage in selective assassinations – something that with the marvels of modern science and technology governments could almost certainly do more easily and less expensively than by pitting armies against armies. It would, moreover, force government leaders to bear directly the major risk for their policies, which today they do not. It might even cause them to be a shade more careful in the setting of those policies. As it is, government leaders stand the least chance of being killed in the event of war, since they do not do the fighting and have their hideaways to enable them to maintain command even if the rest of the country is devastated.[6]

Who has preached the loudest against assassination? National leaders, of course. Civilized countries, they say, don't go around killing individuals like savages do. Instead, we kill people wholesale rather than retail, the innocent along with, or instead of, the guilty.

Obviously, assassination is not intrinsically desirable. What we need is a way to identify, apprehend, and punish those individuals who are causing mischief in the world. What we need, in short, is world government. But if we can't get there right away, if we must continue to use violence to settle human disputes, let's at least do away with the myth that we are punishing nations. What we are doing is killing people, and we should try to point the gun at the right people.

Nations are not persons.

12 Utilitarianism for the family

It is a great mistake for a moral theory to treat everyone as being of equal value to everyone else.

It is right, of course, to treat everyone as being of equal value in the abstract, for there are no privileged persons in moral theory, just as there are no privileged coordinate systems in physical theory. Yet there is a difference in the value each person has from each personal viewpoint, just as there is a difference in the velocity each object has from the viewpoint of each physical coordinate system. And neither of these shifts in value, it should be emphasized, is subjectivistic – both are objective and law-governed.

It is, let us hope, sufficiently established in modern moral theory that every person is important and has value. The point that is generally ignored in ethics is that not every person is equal in importance to everyone else. Even within a family we observe a rough natural progression in perceived value. Each of us tends naturally to value first our spouses, then our children, then parents, grandparents, aunts and uncles, cousins, great-aunts and uncles, second and third cousins, etc., in some such order. (I would be interested to hear if anthropologists have established measures of social closeness, and how they might vary between cultures, but the specific details are of no importance here.) Each of us also tends to behave *in practice* as if our moral obligations decline with this social distance. Our duty to our parents is clearly stronger than that to our cousins, and so on down the line.

Although some might attempt to explain this phenomenon in terms of institutional values or implicit promises, I believe that W. D. Ross came much closer to the truth when he said that some persons stand in special relationships to us and are therefore entitled to *prima facie* consideration.[1] While Ross did not elaborate on these special relationships and their ordering, it seems to me that our duty to others diminishes as a function of social distance along roughly this scale: self, natural family, friends, profession, neighborhood, city, state or region, nation, cultural group, world, rational beings, other animate beings, plants, things. Clearly there are many ways this list could be disputed: the items may not be all-inclusive; they may be in the wrong order; the grouping may not be linear at all but in some way multi-dimensional – again, the details are less important than the concept.

It is my thesis that our duty to others does in fact decline as social distance increases along *some* scale of this sort, or some intuitive sense of social distance. (I am inclined to believe that the moral ordering relationship is also asymmetrical as a function of social well-being, so that Rawls is correct on the general point that our duty is stronger to the least advantaged members of society than to others,[2] and we are also right to feel that we have greater obligations to persons worse off than ourselves and weaker obligations to those who are better off, but nothing crucial to the present point hangs on this.)

The only cases I can recall where great philosophers have taken seriously something like social distance have been Ross's special relationships, and F. H. Bradley's essay, 'My station and its duties.'[3] It could possibly be argued that Bentham's 'propinquity' addresses the issue,[4] but I think not, and he certainly did not spell it out. Sidgwick recognized special duties, but believed they were sufficiently accounted for by the principle of utility.[5] A variety of more contemporary writers have noticed the phenomenon, but none have spelled it out quite the way I see it.[6]

My thesis, put contentiously, is that it is our duty to love our neighbors, not quite as much as ourselves, but more than foreigners. Thus baldly stated, it seems vaguely immoral, certainly egocentric, and presumptively discriminatory. Can a liberal Democrat like me really mean to argue that my white-skinned suburban neighbors are morally more important than dark-skinned foreigners? Is American jingoism recrudescent?

The answer, of course, is that I am not claiming that race has anything to do with it (it is specifically *not* one of the factors on my scale, or any scale I would consider). Neither am I claiming that my neighbors (of whatever color) are *intrinsically* more valuable than foreigners (of whatever color) – I am merely claiming that they loom larger on my moral horizon and consequently *should* receive more weight in *my* moral considerations.

The alternative view – that each person is of equal moral value to every other person – while the received view of most standard ethical theories is, it seems to me, patently unrealistic and never *in practice* accepted by anyone but saints. As I believe that sainthood is supererogatory and can never be a duty, it follows that it cannot be our duty to give equal moral consideration to every person.

Specifically, it cannot be my duty to sell all that I have and give to the poor in Bangladesh. Nobody actually *believes* this is my duty since nobody *does* it, yet utilitarianism implies (especially together with the diminishing marginal utility of wealth) and Christianity asserts that it *is* my duty.[7] (This of course puts Christianity in direct opposition to nationalism – a fact that seems to have escaped jingoistic clerics in many nations.)[8]

While I have not space enough to enter into meta-ethical debate, the Harvard Paradigm convinces me that any moral theory that implies that 99 percent of us constantly live in gross violation of our clear moral duty is probably not a true moral theory. Thus I reject the received view that our duty to each individual is the same as our duty to every other individual.

Nevertheless, we must have *some* duties to socially distant individuals. There is no room in the emerging world society for the provincialism of 'Me and my wife, my son John and his wife, us four, and no more.' What we need is a compromise between the obviously false view that we have no duty to distant people and the obviously impractical (and presumably false) view that our duty to everyone is equal. What we need, in short, is an attenuating device that will permit us to say that our (real) duty to distant people is less strong than our duty to near people. For this role I propose the concept of social distance.

Our duties, then, are not all the same. Each of us is the center of a moral universe that differs from all the others. Our duties are, pre-eminently, *our* duties, not someone else's.[9]

It follows, of course, that our greatest duty is to ourselves.

So far from finding this to be an embarrassment, I believe it is exactly right. The essential truth of ethical egoism and the source of its perennial appeal to sophomoric philosophers is this: my greatest duty *is* to myself. The fundamental mistake of egoism is believing that this one great truth exhausts the moral universe.

This is a simple fact: everyone is important to me, but I am more important than anyone else. This is a principle we live by daily. It is a necessary part of living an individualistic life. It is essential to living any life honestly in a world where other human beings are starving to death. Is your life not more important than the lives of Ethiopian children? Then it *is* your duty to starve yourself in order to save two of their lives. I do not believe this. You do not believe this. Yet most of our moral theories proclaim that it is so. Rather than accept this absurdity, some philosophers have gone to the opposite extreme and denied that we have *any* duty to these children. Isn't it obvious that the solution is that we have *some* duty to preserve and improve their lives but a *greater* duty to preserve and improve our own lives? Is it so shameful to admit this?

Kant, of course, argued that it *is* our duty to preserve our own life (indeed, self-regarding duties are one way in which he viewed the categorical imperative as distinct from, and superior to, the Golden Rule), but that we have only an indirect duty to make ourselves happy (not that the absence of a direct duty to pursue personal happiness makes much difference to human behavior, as Kant also argues that we have an inescapable *desire* for such happiness and will pursue it for other than moral reasons).[10]

Classical utilitarianism does, in contrast, proclaim our duty to make ourselves happy – it just says we have an equivalent duty to everyone else in the universe. In the phrase Mill attributes to Bentham: 'everybody to count for one, nobody for more than one.'[11]

For Bentham's purposes this is true and sufficient, as he was primarily concerned with social engineering within a given society, and, from this perspective, he got it right. But according to Mill and most later utilitarians, Bentham's dictum is to be used not only in its proper sphere of legislation, but also in the 'estimation of the moralist.' As Mill puts it, this 'equal claim of everybody to happiness in the estimation of the moralist and of the legislator, involves an equal claim to all the means of happiness, except in so far as the inevitable conditions of human life, and the general interest, in which that of every individual is included, set limits to the maxim.'[12] Thus our calculations of personal duty are to be conducted in exactly the same manner as our evaluation of social policies.

But our individual duties are *not* miniaturizations of our social ideals – they are ineluctably individual. In my world I am special. In your world you are special. In *the* world we are equal, but our *duties* are not equal. Your duty is to improve your little corner of the world, and mine is similarly focussed (though not circumscribed) to the part of the world I inhabit.[13] In reacting against the utilitarian view that we are all morally interchangeable parts, W. D. Ross undertook to list the different relations we may have to others and the corresponding general types of *prima facie* duties to which we are subject.[14] The 'special relations' invoked are : promisor to promisee; converser to converser; injurer to injured; recipient to benefactor; enforcer of justice to victim of injustice; potential benefactor to potential beneficiary; improving self to imperfect self; potential malefactor to potential victim. The notions of 'neighbor,' 'wife,' 'husband,' 'child,' 'parent,' 'friend,' 'fellow countryman,' and the like, which had been discussed earlier, are not explicitly mentioned in this catalog of duties. There is also no provision for gradation or attenuation of relations within categories. I conclude, therefore, that Ross shared my view that our duties to others are, in general, not equal, but he did not develop anything like my concept of social distance.

If we deny that our duties to others are unequal, if we try seriously to be Christians or utilitarians, for example, without giving special weight to ourselves, our friends, and our families, it becomes immediately obvious that there would be more happiness in the world if, for example, my sports car were sacrificed to meet the basic needs of distant others. Many moralists and social reformers have drawn this conclusion about the conspicuous consumption of the rich; few have had the honesty or hardihood to see that the very same principles apply to the modest pleasures of the middle class.

If everyone is equally the object of our moral duty, we are indeed sinning every time we use more than the irreducible minimum of the world's resources required to maintain our own existence (and possibly even then, if we are not among the most productive members of society). This cannot be true, or the human race is even more sinful than Calvin believed. As Bradley remarked, it leads to 'a standing contradiction which [brings] with it a perpetual self-deceit, or the depressing perpetual confession that I am not what I ought to be in my inner heart, and that I never can be so.'[15] There must be some way to recognize our duty to others without being morally overwhelmed by their claims on us.

The situation is this: if I have an asset that would make any other persons happier than it makes me, most orthodox moral views imply that it is my duty to give it all to them. I deny this theoretically, while most of the rest of the world denies it only in practice.[16] Ethical egoists, on the other extreme, make the greater moral mistake of denying that I have any moral responsibility to those other persons at all.

When considering our duties to the rest of the human family, we find that most traditional views are doubly inadequate. In theory, they make our duty too strong to be met, while in practice, they treat our universal duty as too weak to amount to much.

On my view, on the other hand, our duty is one of gradual amelioration that diminishes but does not vanish with social distance. Those of us who enjoy a reasonably comfortable life *do* have a duty to end the starvation in Bangladesh, but it does not override our duty to improve the lives of our well-to-do neighbors. The two are not directly commensurable, until social distance is factored in. Even then I believe that they are not exchangeable, so that one can negate the other by its greater importance. Rather, just as Rawls criticized utilitarianism for failing to take seriously the difference between persons,[17] I believe we should take seriously the difference between social contexts. In each context, it is our duty to make that part of the world a better place. It does not follow that it is our duty to make Paris a *worse* place in order to make Africa a better place.

Here the insights of negative utilitarianism and the physician's creed are important: first do no harm. For each individual in the world, in each social context, it is our duty not to harm that individual – but it is not our duty to help *that* individual.

Using negative utilitarianism as the touchstone of duty likewise addresses the Rawlsian concern that classical utilitarianism would sacrifice the well-being of some in order to improve the lives of others.[18] Negative utilitarians, counting only the pain, would allow some to suffer only to prevent the greater suffering of others, which is certainly less objectionable than buying happiness through the pain of a few.

Likewise, the combination of negative utilitarianism and the concept of social distance accounts for the natural human feeling that we have a duty not to harm (unnecessarily) other animals, but that duty is strongest with those animals that most resemble us (chimpanzees, dolphins, dogs, horses) and weakest for those that differ from us the most (worms, ants, bacteria).

The place of positive utilitarianism, I believe, is principally in the assessment of our moral worth. It gives the value of our lives, in terms of what we have contributed to the world. Yet, once again, it is more important that our own child is happy and well developed than our neighbors'; we get more points for behaving decently to our colleagues at work than for giving to charity; we are judged primarily by our own lives and how we affect those around us.

Social distance is not just a fact of nature, or a deplorable practical complication in ethics, it is a fundamentally important moral consideration. If we are to live at peace as a human family, we must each do our part, and we must each care for all the others; but no one has to do everything, and no one can love everyone equally. It will suffice if we each try to make our part of the world a better place and have a little fun doing it.

13 Conclusion: a family at peace

We find ourselves in a world divided and at war. Some wars are based on greed; some on political grievances. But an appalling and disgraceful number spring from nationalism, religious differences, and other forms of bigotry that dehumanize the enemy and treat them as non-persons.

Some wars are tribal in scope; some so diminutive as to be properly called feuds. But the wars that matter, the wars that represent one of the greatest sins of, by, and against humanity, are the wars between nations.

I feel about nationalism as Marx felt about capitalism – it was necessary, even good, in its time, but it has no place in a mature human society. Nationalism expanded the web of social cooperation by extending the title of 'citizen' to great numbers of people. This, in itself and in its pure consequences, is a good thing. But nationalism achieves its good end by the pernicious device of blocking out others, denying their equal worth, ultimately denying them personhood and taking up arms against them.

The negative condition requisite for the elimination of war is the elimination of national sovereignty and the 'right' of nations to make war against each other.

The positive condition requisite for the attainment of true peace is the development of a broader conception of personhood, embracing all persons who live in the world and, ultimately, in the universe, as members of the human family.

Both the end of war and the development of the human family depend strongly on the creation of an effective world government. Conflicts between nations are now resolved by force all too often. This would not happen if (a) alternative means of conflict resolution were available, and (b) nations could ultimately be forced to accept these alternative means and be prohibited from engaging in violence. This is how disputes between individuals, families, townships, cities, counties, provinces, and states are currently settled, and no one would have it any other way. Why, then, do so many fail to extend the same logic to the resolution of conflicts between nations?

Nationalism continues to flourish for many reasons, most of them bad. Chief among them are bigotry, xenophobia, greed, and insecurity. There are only two intellectually and morally respectable arguments against the development of world government that I can see, and both of them are wrong.

It is said, first of all, that development of a world state would diminish the cultural diversity of the world and this would be a bad thing. I agree that it would somewhat diminish cultural diversity, but I deny that this would be a bad thing – because the parts of their culture that people surrender peacefully are, on pain of an irrational conception of humanity, the parts that they see as less desirable than what replaces them. They will always have *some* form of culture. They have the right and the option to reject any parts of the world culture they find unacceptable. We should not force them to continue in cultures where their lives are 'solitary, poor, nasty, brutish and short.'[1]

Fortunately, the forces of history are working in my favor.

World culture is being developed before our very eyes, by education, travel, and communication on a scale never seen before. A world language is evolving, not by decree or even democratic agreement, but organically, socially, economically, and by the free choice of each individual involved. Granted, humanity does not always do the rational thing, or do it in a timely manner. But the rationality, the convenience, the *necessity* of a world language is becoming so evident that millions are working to learn it, and their efforts will become progressively easier as the world language spreads more and more into global communication, economic activity, political intercourse, and entertainment.

The world language, barring unforeseen cataclysmic developments, will be English. I base this claim on no pretense whatsoever that English is a 'better' language than any other (it is, for example, more complex and less systematic than most). Nor do I claim that English-speaking cultures are in any clear sense 'better' cultures than others in the world. (Although in many pair-wise comparisons I would in fact make this claim, my main point does not depend on it.)

The reason English will become the world language is that it happened to be at center stage when the world became ready for a world language. This is largely due to the dominance of the United States as a military, economic, and entertainment superpower, but there are other historical convergences at work as well (witness the academic conference conducted in English with no thought of appeasing or imitating the US – it just made sense because English is *already* so well established as the dominant *second* language of the world).

Along with world culture and world language, there is a weaker but discernible trend towards world government. The most important exemplar is the unification of Europe. If the mature, long-standing nations of Europe succeed in eliminating national sovereignty in favor of the sovereignty of the European Community, it will serve as a powerful example to the rest of the world, and a powerful economic incentive as well. Once the point has been clearly made that national boundaries are an inefficient anachronism, the rest will follow.

In addition, the collapse of the Soviet Union and the tremendous (if, as yet, partial) success of democracy around the world augur well for the fundamental good sense of humanity and for our undying love of freedom. This, too, will serve as an important teaching point: when national and multinational tyrannies are brought down, it tends to reduce the reasonable fear (and the actual possibility) that a world government might become despotic.

Eventually, the world will be governed by a branching hierarchy of governments, each appropriate to its own sphere of influence and level of generality, each responsible to the democratic vote of its citizens and each subordinate to the next higher level on matters – and *only* on matters – appropriately governed by that level.

And what of the individual in this peaceful world family? Each of us will indeed be subject to a system of legal rules and regulations, but they will be rules we have helped develop, and we will be free to move to other governmental areas if they suit us better. Some of our old rights – especially property rights – will diminish or disappear. But our actual wealth and our average power to *do* things (as opposed to merely *owning* things) will be greatly increased. Computers and robots will free us from much of the tyranny of labor, and will make possible new forms of creativity and production. Our *personal* freedoms will be virtually unrestricted, subject only to the requirement that we do not harm anyone else.

And, finally, our moral vision will be revised. By seeing the world as the home of the human family we will come to value the world and all its occupants far more highly than did our predecessors. But our moral vision will recognize a new way of conceptualizing our obligations. For the first time, each individual will count equally before the law, regardless of race, color, creed, gender, sexual preference, or national origin. Each individual will also be equally protected from harm by moral proscriptions – moral *pre*scriptions, however, will be substantially revised.

No more will we be told that we have an equal positive duty to all human beings. No more will we be commanded to sell all we have and give to the poor, and made to feel guilty when (inevitably) we fail to comply. Instead, we will recognize our family duties to humanity. We will be most concerned with those in our immediate family, and will love, succor, and support them more than we do the rest of the world, and we will be right in doing so. We will seek to improve our corner of the world first, and devote more energy to making happy the people we encounter in daily life than those who live far away in the rain forests, and we will be right in doing so. But we *will* recognize that those distant relatives have *some* claim on us, so we will structure our governments and our economies to gradually lessen the gap – not by forcibly impoverishing the middle class, nor even by expropriating the wealth of the plutocrats, but by a gradual policy of progressive taxation and Rawlsian downward transfers we will structure our world to place far more *systematic, collective* effort into improving the lot of the least-advantaged than we have ever done before.

Every family has rich uncles and poor relations. So long as conditions of moderate scarcity persist, most of us will continue to feel that that's as it should be. For a variety of reasons, a policy of differential rewards seems to fit into our view of things. But the day is quickly coming when we will no longer be able to tolerate starvation, war, pestilence, or a lack of medical care anywhere in our human family.

We have eliminated smallpox and slavery from the human condition, thus proving that human suffering is *not* inevitable and that we *can* conquer the ancient evils of the earth. Tyranny is now in retreat, and may yet be gone by the end of this century. World war, I believe, is behind us already, and national warfare will be eliminated by the end of the next century. The elimination of poverty depends in part on the control of the world's population, which may in turn depend on the attenuation of religiosity, but both processes are under way already. It is not unrealistic to think that grinding poverty at the starvation level will be completely eliminated by the end of the twenty-second century, and the human family will live in harmonious peace and prosperity.

For those who find this prospect morally satisfying but personally boring, we have a universe to explore!

Notes

1 World peace as an ideal

1 But for a fascinating and scholarly criticism of this standard view, see J. T. Johnson, *The Quest for Peace*, Princeton, NJ, Princeton University Press, 1987, pp. 3–47.
2 Matthew 10.34.
3 E. Balch, *Beyond Nationalism: Social Thought of Emily Greene Balch*, ed. M. Randall, New York, Twayne Publishers, 1972, p. 220.
4 K. Marx and F. Engels, 'Manifesto of the Communist Party,' trans. by S. Moore in 1888 from the original German text of 1848 and edited by F. Engels, reprinted in J. A. Gould (ed.) *Classic Philosophical Questions*, 5th edition, Columbus, Ohio, Charles A. Merrill, 1985, p. 596.
5 K. Marx, *Critique of the Gotha Programme*, written and privately circulated in 1875, published by Engels in 1891, reprinted Peking, Foreign Languages Press, 1972, p. 17.
6 F. H. Bradley, 'Essay V: My station and its duties,' in F. H. Bradley, *Ethical Studies*, Oxford, Clarendon Press, 1927, p. 181.
7 Johnson, op. cit., pp. xi–xii.
8 ibid., p. xiv.
9 ibid.

10 I would like to thank Hilary Putnam for pointing this out to me. When I told him about this project, the first thing he said was 'Re-read Kant's *Perpetual Peace*, and this time take it seriously.'

11 I. Kant, *Perpetual Peace*, Indianapolis, Bobbs-Merrill, 1957 (1795), p. 10n.

12 S. Genoves, *Is Peace Inevitable?*, New York, Walker, 1970, p. 88.

2 World peace as a possibility

1 O. White, 'Nations not fighting each other, yet civil wars taking huge toll,' *St. Petersburg Times*, January 16, 1992.

2 H. Kohn, 'A new look at nationalism,' in U. G. Whitaker (ed.) *Nationalism and International Progress*, San Francisco, Chandler, 1960, p. 23.

3 Although to be sure, many such new citizens were created for the express purpose of becoming Roman soldiers. See J. T. Johnson, *The Quest for Peace*, Princeton, NJ, Princeton University Press, 1987, pp. 34–35.

4 E. Balch, *Beyond Nationalism: Social Thought of Emily Greene Balch*, ed. M. Randall, New York, Twayne Publishers, 1972, p. 220.

5 F. H. Hinsley, *Nationalism and the International System*, Dobbs Ferry, NY, Oceana Publications, 1973, p. 5. (Editor's Preface, D. Tyerman.)

6 ibid., p. 80.

7 ibid., p. 11.

8 ibid., p. 19.

9 ibid., p. 20.

10 ibid., p. 21.

11 I. Kant, *Perpetual Peace*, Indianapolis, Bobbs-Merrill, 1957 (1795), p. 23.

12 For a discussion of the problems created by new and emerging nations, see P. Calvocoressi, *World Order and New States*, New York, Frederick A. Praeger, 1962.

13 D. Ross, unpublished private communication, 1991.

14 John 12.8.
15 Balch, op. cit., p. 184.
16 Hinsley, op. cit., p. 67.
17 E. M. Chaney, 'Migrant workers and national boundaries: the basis for rights and protections,' chapter 2 in P. G. Brown and H. Shue (eds) *Boundaries: National Autonomy and its Limits*, Totowa, NJ, Rowman & Littlefield, 1981, p. 58.
18 E. de Vattel, *The Law of Nations or the Principles of Natural Law: Applied to the Conduct and to the Affairs of Nations and of Sovereigns*, cited in R. L. Holmes, *On War and Morality*, Princeton, Princeton University Press, 1989, p. 158.
19 Kant rejected Vattel's views, employing the running pun on 'perpetual peace' as either the peace of the League of Nations or the peace of the grave:

> The concept of a law of nations as a right to make war does not really mean anything, because it is then a law of deciding what is right by unilateral maxims through force and not by universally valid public laws which restrict the freedom of each one. The only conceivable meaning of such a law of nations might be that it serves men right who are so inclined that they should destroy each other and thus find perpetual peace in the vast grave that swallows both the atrocities and their perpetrators. For states in their relations to each other, there cannot be any reasonable way out of the lawless condition which entails only war except that they, like individual men, should give up their savage (lawless) freedom, adjust themselves to the constraints of public law, and thus establish a continuously growing state consisting of various nations (*civitas gentium*), which will ultimately include all the nations of the world.
>
> (Kant, op. cit., p. 19)

20 Hinsley, op. cit., pp. 116–117.

21 ibid., pp. 123–124.
22 ibid., p. 134.
23 Kant, op. cit., pp. 31–32.
24 Calvocoressi, op. cit., pp. 2–3.
25 D. Weatherford, *Encyclopedia of the History of American Women*, New York, Prentice-Hall, forthcoming.
26 Hinsley, op. cit., p. 143.

3 World peace as an institution

1 C. J. H. Hayes, 'Nationalism – curse or blessing?,' in U. G. Whitaker (ed.) *Nationalism and International Progress*, San Francisco, Chandler, 1960, pp. 201–2.
2 I. Kant, *Perpetual Peace*, Indianapolis, Bobbs-Merrill, 1957 (1795), p. 16.
3 H. Morgenthau, 'Nationalism: dilemma,' in U. G. Whitaker (ed.) *Nationalism and International Progress*, San Francisco, Chandler, 1960, p. 190.
4 Kant, op. cit., pp. 7–8.
5 P. Calvocoressi, *World Order and New States*, New York, Frederick A. Praeger, 1962, p. 72.
6 L. L. Snyder, *Macro-Nationalisms: A History of the Pan-Movements*, Westport, Conn., Greenwood Press, 1984, p. 66.
7 ibid., p. 254.
8 See especially H. Tamashiro, G. G. Brunk and D. Secrest, 'The underlying structure of ethical beliefs toward war,' *Journal of Peace Research*, vol. 26, no. 2, 1989, pp. 147–50, for the risk-aversive characteristics of military officers.
9 In a private discussion at the USF Faculty Club, May 28, 1992.
10 H. Mitchell, 'The perils of power, in war and in peace,' *The Washington Post*, January 18, 1991, p. C2.
11 E. Laucks, 'The transitional family,' in C. C. Barbeau (ed.) *The Future of the Family*, New York, Bruce Publishing, 1971, p. 76.

4 The human family as an ideal

1 As someone has 'borrowed' my Brother Dave records, I am not presently able to give an exact citation for this remark. I believe it was on the album *Kick thine own self.* In any event, those who care to find it will have a wonderful time sifting through his sometimes outrageous and often philosophical, but always funny, comedy routines.

2 E. Laucks, 'The transitional family,' in C. C. Barbeau (ed.) *The Future of the Family*, New York, Bruce Publishing, 1971, p. 68.

5 The human family as a possibility

1 E. Shorter, *The Making of the Modern Family*, New York, Basic Books, 1975, p. 206.

2 E. Balch, *Beyond Nationalism: Social Thought of Emily Greene Balch*, ed. M. Randall, New York, Twayne Publishers, 1972, p. 184.

3 Shorter, op. cit., pp. 258–259.

4 W. J. Goode, *World Revolution and Family Patterns*, London, Free Press of Glencoe, 1963, p. 1.

5 ibid., p. 380.

6 See, for example, A. Heraclides, 'Conflict resolution, ethnonationalism and the Middle East impasse,' *Journal of Peace Research*, vol. 26, no. 2, 1989, pp. 197–212, for a discussion of the roots and imperatives of ethnic rebellions.

6 The human family as an institution

1 K. Marx, *Critique of the Gotha Programme*, written in 1875, edited and first published by F. Engels in 1891, reprinted by Foreign Languages Press, Peking, 1972.

2 This is an approximation from memory. The show in general does a good job of exploring social and philo-

sophical themes – notably questions of personhood (is the android Commander Data a machine or a person?) and moral obligation (is Commander Worf still obliged to support the Klingon empire when its goals conflict with those of the Federation?).

3 R. Rodgers and O. Hammerstein, II, 'Carefully taught,' from the musical *South Pacific*, Columbia Masterworks, OS 2040.

7 Economic interdependence

1 I. Kant, *Perpetual Peace*, Indianapolis, Bobbs-Merrill, 1957 (1795), p. 32.

2 T. J. Biersteker, 'Conclusion,' in P. G. Brown and H. Shue (eds) *Boundaries: National Autonomy and its Limits*, Totowa, NJ, Rowman & Littlefield, 1981, p. 170.

3 Reuters, 'World Bank: governments need role in free markets,' *St. Petersburg Times*, July 8, 1991, p. 10A.

4 World Bank Chief Economist Lawrence Summers, quoted ibid.

8 Cultural interdependence

1 C. J. H. Hayes, 'Bases of nationalism,' in U. G. Whitaker (ed.) *Nationalism and International Progress*, San Francisco, Chandler, 1960, p. 7.

2 F. Hellerman and F. Minkoff, 'Poverty Hill,' performed by the Kingston Trio on their eponymous album, *The Kingston Trio*, Decca, DL 74613.

3 K. Marx and F. Engels, 'Manifesto of the Communist Party,' trans. by S. Moore in 1888 from the original German text of 1848 and edited by F. Engels, reprinted in J. A. Gould (ed.) *Classic Philosophical Questions*, Columbus, Ohio, Charles E. Merrill, 1985.

4 This and subsequent statistics on world population and language distribution are taken from *The World Almanac*

and Book of Facts, New York, Newspaper Enterprise Association, 1985 and 1991 editions.

5 D. Yerkes, 'English language,' *Academic American Encyclopedia*, electronic version, 1992.

6 Professor R. O'Hara, during his television course on linguistics at the University of South Florida, Fall semester 1991.

7 Yerkes, op. cit., emphasis added.

8 This, oddly enough, *is* a quote from an eminent contemporary philosopher. When I was discussing with Rogers Albritton my intention to drop out of graduate school and perform my required military service, Professor Albritton, then chair of the Philosophy Department at Harvard, astonished me by saying that he thought I would enjoy my tour in the Army; he certainly had. Skeptically, I asked him if he liked it so much, why he got out. 'Oh, well,' he said, 'you can't stay in kindergarten forever.'

9 Environmental interdependence

1 E. T. Freyfogle, 'Environment requires a new idea of property,' *St. Petersburg Times*, January 4, 1982, p. 17A.

2 H. Shue, 'Exporting hazards,' in P. G. Brown and H. Shue (eds), *Boundaries: National Autonomy and its Limits*, Totowa, NJ, Rowman & Littlefield, 1981, p. 116.

3 J. Lichtenberg, 'National boundaries and moral boundaries: a cosmopolitan view,' ibid., pp. 85–86. The clause 'the limits of the planet are the limits of our world' is followed by a footnote citing C. F. Bergsten, 'Coming investment wars?' *Foreign Affairs*, vol. 53, no. 1, 1974, p. 137.

4 W. Quine, 'Two dogmas of empiricism,' *Philosophical Review*, 1951, reprinted in W. Quine, *From a Logical Point of View: 9 Logico-Philosophical Essays*, Cambridge, Mass., Harvard University Press, 1980 (1953), p. 46.

5 S. and P. Scharper, 'The futures of the family,' in C. C.

Barbeau (ed.) *The Future of the Family*, New York, Bruce Publishing, 1971, pp. 108–109.

11 Who is a person?

1 I. Vine, 'The nature of moral commitments,' chapter 2 in H. Weinrich-Haste and D. Locke (eds) *Morality in the Making: Thought, Action, and the Social Context*, Chichester and New York, John Wiley, 1983, p. 30.
2 M. Walzer, 'The distribution of membership,' in P. Brown and H. Shue (eds) *Boundaries: National Autonomy and its Limits*, Totowa, NJ, Rowman & Littlefield, 1981, pp. 7–8.
3 G. M. Breakwell, 'Moralities and conflicts,' chapter 13 in Weinrich-Haste and Locke, op. cit., pp. 239–40.
4 See C. R. Beitz, *Political Theory and International Relations*, Princeton, NJ, Princeton University Press, 1979, for a clear exposition and important critique of these alternative traditional views.
5 N. Machiavelli, *The Prince*, in vol. 36 of *The Harvard Classics*, New York, P. F. Collier, 1910 (1512–13), especially chapters XV–XVIII.
6 R. L. Holmes, *On War and Morality*, Princeton, NJ, Princeton University Press, 1989, p. 262.

12 Utilitarianism for the family

1 W. D. Ross, *The Right and the Good*, Oxford, Clarendon Press, 1930, p. 19.
2 J. Rawls, *A Theory of Justice*, Cambridge, Mass., Harvard University Press, 1971, pp. 90–100. See also my 'Defining the least advantaged,' *The Philosophical Quarterly*, vol. 33, no. 130, January 1983, pp. 63–70, reprinted in J. A. Corlett (ed.) *Equality and Liberty*, London, Macmillan, 1991, pp. 37–45.
3 F. H. Bradley, 'My station and its duties,' in *Ethical*

Studies, Oxford, Clarendon Press, 2nd edition, 1927, pp. 160–213.

4 J. Bentham, *An Introduction to the Principles of Morals and Legislation*, in *The Utilitarians*, Garden City, NY, Doubleday, 1961 (1823), p. 37.

5 H. Sidgwick, *The Methods of Ethics*, New York, Macmillan, 1907 (1874), bk. 4, ch. 3.

6 Judith Lichtenberg perhaps comes closest to my view when she says:

> This is not to say that human beings could ever be equally committed to all other human beings, or that this is even abstractly desirable. The question is where the crucial dividing lines are that mark off levels and qualities of a person's capacity for commitment. The most crucial such line seems to be between those with whom one has face-to-face relations and those with whom one does not. One could not be expected, nor would it be desirable to try, to treat those whom one sees and knows just as one treats those whom one does not. We may in this way set off family and tribal loyalty. (J. Lichtenberg, 'National boundaries and moral boundaries: a cosmopolitan view,' in P. G. Brown and H. Shue (eds) *Boundaries: National Autonomy and its Limits*, Totowa, NJ, Rowman & Littlefield, 1981, pp. 96–7).

L. C. Becker, *Reciprocity*, London, Routledge & Kegan Paul, 1986, presents an impressive and well-argued view that our moral duties are at least in part a function of our special relation to certain other persons, and bases these special relations on the notion of reciprocity. R. E. Goodin, *Protecting the Vulnerable: A Reanalysis of Our Social Responsibilities*, Chicago and London, University of Chicago Press, 1985, p. xi, uses a similar form of argument but focusses on the relation of vulnerability. Becker actually uses the term 'social distance' in much the same way that I, independently, had settled on using it.

T. Kitwood, while arguing in favor of recognizing non-universal moral duties, also does a good job of citing some of the dangers, including 'the risk of providing the legitimation for many kinds of special pleading, for corruption in public life, for the labelling of non-members as sub-human and therefore outside the scope of ethical concern: indeed, for modern versions of the very kinds of practice that the early utilitarians were opposing. Ultimately we might be giving grounds for justifying the social system of fascism itself' (in ' "Personal identity" and personal integrity,' chapter 12 in H. Weinrich-Haste, and D. Locke (eds) *Morality in the Making: Thought, Action, and the Social Context*, Chichester and New York, John Wiley, 1983, pp. 226–227.

7 Matthew 19.21; Mark 10.21.

8 'Yet nationalism embodies more than merely the natural and universal sentiment of devotion to one's own kin, language, culture and plot of land. By identification of nation and state, nationalism is the expression of an absolute, exclusive devotion to one's country. It refuses to recognise the common bond of humanity; it is the antithesis to the Christian concept of the brotherhood of all men; it is the sentiment of extended selfishness which sets the nation above every moral law. Every nationalism is guided by the principle: "My country, right or wrong." ' (J. Braunthal, 'The moral paradox of nationalism,' in U. G. Whitaker (ed.) *Nationalism and International Progress*, San Francisco, Chandler, 1960, p. 192.)

9 Bradley says my duty is 'mine and no other man's' (op. cit., p. 162), and 'to know what a man is (as we have seen) you must not take him in isolation. He is one of a people, he was born in a family, he lives in a certain society, in a certain state. What he has to do depends on what his place is, what his function is, and that all

comes from his station in the organism' (F. H. Bradley, op. cit., p. 173).

10 I. Kant, *Foundations of the Metaphysics of Morals*, translated and with an introduction by L. W. Beck, Indianapolis, Bobbs-Merrill, 1959 (1785), pp. 14–15, and *Critique of Practical Reason*, translated by L. W. Beck, Indianapolis, Bobbs-Merrill, 1956 (1788), p. 24 and p. 36.

11 J. S. Mill, *Utilitarianism*, Indianapolis, Bobbs-Merrill, 1957 (1863), p. 76.

12 ibid., pp. 76–77.

13 Bradley again: 'It is not wrong, it is a duty, standing on the basis of the existing, and in harmony with its general spirit, to try and make not only oneself but also the world better, or rather, and in preference, one's own world better' (op. cit., p. 200).

And Ross:

> The essential defect of the 'ideal utilitarian' theory is that it ignores, or at least does not do full justice to, the highly personal character of duty. If the only duty is to produce the maximum of good, the question who is to have the good – whether it is myself, or my benefactor, or a person to whom I have made a promise to confer that good on him, or a mere fellow man to whom I stand in no such special relation – should make no difference to my having a duty to produce that good. But we are all in fact sure that it makes a vast difference (op. cit., p. 22).

And Goodin: 'Duty, even more than charity, begins at home' (op. cit., p. 2).

14 Ross, op. cit., p. 21.

15 Bradley, op. cit., p. 181.

16 An exception is Bradley, who says that

> In 'duty for duty's sake' we were always unsatisfied, no nearer our goal at the end than at the beginning.

There we had the fixed antithesis of the sensuous self on one side and a non-sensuous moral ideal on the other – a standing contradiction which brought with it a perpetual self-deceit, or the depressing perpetual confession that I am not what I ought to be in my inner heart, and that I never can be so. Duty, we thus saw, was an infinite process, an unending 'not-yet'; a continual 'not' with an everlasting 'to be', or an abiding 'to be' with a ceaseless 'not'.

From this last peevish enemy we are again delivered by 'my station and its duties'. There I realize myself morally, so that not only what ought to be in the world is, but I am what I ought to be, and find so my contentment and satisfaction. If this were not the case, when we consider that the ordinary moral man is self-contented and happy, we should be forced to accuse him of immorality, and we do not do this; we say he most likely might be better, but we do not say that he is bad, or need consider himself so. Why is this? It is because 'my station and its duties' teaches us to identify others and ourselves with the station we fill; to consider that as good, and by virtue of that to consider others and ourselves good too. It teaches us that a man who does his work in the world is good, notwithstanding his faults, if his faults do not prevent him from fulfilling his station (op. cit., p. 181).

17 Rawls, op. cit., pp. 26–30, 187–189.
18 ibid., p. 180.

13 Conclusion: a family at peace

1 T. Hobbes, *Leviathan*, chapter 13, in T. Smith and M. Grene (eds) *Philosophers Speak for Themselves: From Descartes to Locke*, Chicago, Phoenix Books, University of Chicago Press, 1957 (1940) (1650), p. 191.

Select bibliography

Balch, E., *Beyond Nationalism: Social Thought of Emily Greene Balch*, ed. M. Randall, New York, Twayne Publishers, 1972.

Barbeau, C. C. (ed.) *The Future of the Family*, New York, Bruce Publishing, 1971.

Becker, L. C., *Reciprocity*, London, Routledge & Kegan Paul, 1986.

Beitz, C., *Political Theory and International Relations*, Princeton, Princeton University Press, 1979.

Bentham, J., *An Introduction to the Principles of Morals and Legislation*, in *The Utilitarians*, Garden City, NY, Dolphin Books, Doubleday, 1961 (1823).

Biersteker, T. J., 'Conclusion,' in P. G. Brown and H. Shue (eds) *Boundaries: National Autonomy and its Limits*, Totowa, NJ, Rowman & Littlefield, 1981.

Bradley, F. H., 'Essay V: My station and its duties,' in F. H. Bradley, *Ethical Studies*, Oxford, Clarendon Press, 1927.

Braunthal, J., 'The moral paradox of nationalism,' in U. G. Whitaker (ed.) *Nationalism and International Progress*, San Francisco, Chandler, 1960.

Breakwell, G. M., 'Moralities and conflicts,' chapter 13 in H. Weinrich-Haste and D. Locke (eds) *Morality in the Making: Thought, Action, and the Social Context*, Chichester and New York, John Wiley, 1983.

Brown, P. G., and Shue, H. (eds) *Boundaries: National Autonomy and its Limits*, Totowa, NJ, Rowman & Littlefield, 1981.

Calvocoressi, P., *World Order and New States*, New York, Frederick A. Praeger, 1962.

Chaney, E. M., 'Migrant workers and national boundaries: the basis for rights and protections,' chapter 2 in P. G. Brown and H. Shue (eds) *Boundaries: National Autonomy and its Limits*, Totowa, NJ, Rowman & Littlefield, 1981.

Corlett, J. A. (ed.) *Equality and Liberty*, London, Macmillan, 1991.
Genoves, S., *Is Peace Inevitable?*, New York, Walker, 1970.
Goode, W. J., *World Revolution and Family Patterns*, London, Free Press of Glencoe, 1963.
Goodin, Robert E., *Protecting the Vulnerable: A Reanalysis of Our Social Responsibilities*, Chicago and London, University of Chicago Press, 1985.
Hayes, C. J. H., 'Bases of nationalism,' in U. G. Whitaker (ed.) *Nationalism and International Progress*, San Francisco, Chandler, 1960.
—, 'Nationalism – curse or blessing?' in U. G. Whitaker (ed.) *Nationalism and International Progress*, San Francisco, Chandler, 1960.
Heraclides, A., 'Conflict resolution, ethnonationalism and the Middle East impasse,' *Journal of Peace Research*, vol. 26, no. 2, 1989, pp. 197–212.
Hinsley, F. H., *Nationalism and the International System*, Dobbs Ferry, NY, Oceana Publications, 1973.
Hobbes, T., *Leviathan*, chapter 13, in T. Smith and M. Grene (eds) *Philosophers Speak for Themselves: From Descartes to Locke*, Chicago, Phoenix Books, University of Chicago Press, 1957 (1940) (1650).
Holmes, R. L., *On War and Morality*, Princeton, NJ, Princeton University Press, 1989.
Holy Bible, Revised Standard Version, New York, Thomas Nelson, 1946.
Johnson, J. T., *The Quest for Peace*, Princeton, NJ, Princeton University Press, 1987.
Kant, I., *Foundations of the Metaphysics of Morals*, translated and with an introduction by L. W. Beck, Indianapolis, Bobbs-Merrill, 1959 (1785).
—, *Critique of Practical Reason*, translated by L. W. Beck, Indianapolis, Bobbs-Merrill, 1956 (1788).
Kitwood, T., ' "Personal identity" and personal integrity,' chapter 12 in H. Weinrich-Haste and D. Locke (eds) *Morality in the Making: Thought, Action, and the Social Context*, Chichester and New York, John Wiley, 1983.
Kohn, H., 'A new look at nationalism,' in U. G. Whitaker (ed.) *Nationalism and International Progress*, San Francisco, Chandler, 1960.
Laucks, E., 'The transitional family,' in C. C. Barbeau (ed.) *The Future of the Family*, New York, Bruce Publishing, 1971.
Lichtenberg, J., 'National boundaries and moral boundaries: a cosmopolitan view,' chapter 3 in P. G. Brown and H. Shue (eds)

Boundaries: National Autonomy and its Limits, Totowa, NJ, Rowman & Littlefield, 1981.

Machiavelli, N., *The Prince*, in vol. 36 of *The Harvard Classics*, New York, P. F. Collier & Son, 1910 (1512/13).

Marx, K., *Critique of the Gotha Programme*, written and privately circulated in 1875, published by Engels in 1891, reprinted Peking, Foreign Languages Press, 1972.

Marx, K., and Engels, F., 'Manifesto of the Communist Party,' trans. by S. Moore in 1888 from the original German text of 1848 and edited by F. Engels, reprinted in J. A. Gould (ed.) *Classic Philosophical Questions*, 5th edition, Columbus, Ohio, Charles A. Merrill, 1985, p. 596.

Mill, J. S., *Utilitarianism*, Indianapolis, Bobbs-Merrill, 1957 (1863).

Mitchell, H., 'The perils of power, in war and in peace,' *The Washington Post*, January 18, 1991, p. C2.

Morgenthau, H., 'Nationalism: dilemma,' in U. G. Whitaker (ed.) *Nationalism and International Progress*, San Francisco, Chandler, 1960.

Quine, W. V. O., 'Two dogmas of empiricism,' *Philosophical Review*, January 1951, reprinted in W. Quine, *From a Logical Point of View: 9 Logico-Philosophical Essays*, Cambridge, Mass., Harvard University Press, 1980 (1953).

Rawls, J., *A Theory of Justice*, Cambridge, Mass., Harvard University Press, 1971.

Reuters, 'World Bank: Governments need role in free markets,' *St. Petersburg Times*, July 8, 1991, p. 10A.

Ross, W. D., *The Right and the Good*, Oxford, Clarendon Press, 1930.

Scharper, S. and P., 'The futures of the family,' in C. C. Barbeau (ed.) *The Future of the Family*, New York, Bruce Publishing, 1971.

Shorter, E., *The Making of the Modern Family*, New York, Basic Books, 1975.

Shue, H., 'Exporting hazards,' in P. G. Brown and H. Shue (eds) *Boundaries: National Autonomy and its Limits*, Totowa, NJ, Rowman & Littlefield, 1981.

Sidgwick, Henry, *The Methods of Ethics*, 7th edition, London, Macmillan, 1907 (1874).

Snyder, L. L., *Macro-Nationalisms: A History of the Pan-Movements*, Westport, Conn., Greenwood Press, 1984.

Tamashiro, H., Brunk, G. G. and Secrest, D., 'The underlying structure of ethical beliefs toward war,' *Journal of Peace Research*, vol. 26, no. 2, 1989, pp. 139–52.

Vine, I., 'The nature of moral commitments,' chapter 2 in H. Weinrich-Haste and D. Locke (eds) *Morality in the Making:*

Thought, Action, and the Social Context, Chichester and New York, John Wiley, 1983.

Walzer, M., 'The distribution of membership,' in P. G. Brown and H. Shue (eds) *Boundaries: National Autonomy and its Limits*, Totowa, NJ, Rowman & Littlefield, 1981, pp. 1–35.

Weatherford, D., *Encyclopedia of the History of American Women*, New York, Prentice-Hall, forthcoming.

Weatherford, R., 'Defining the least advantaged,' *The Philosophical Quarterly*, vol. 33, no. 130, January 1983, pp. 63–70, reprinted in J. A. Corlett (ed.) *Equality and Liberty*, London, Macmillan, 1991, pp. 37–45.

Whitaker, U. G. (ed.) *Nationalism and International Progress*, San Francisco, Chandler, 1960.

White, O., 'Nations not fighting each other, yet civil wars taking huge toll,' *St. Petersburg Times*, January 16, 1992, p. 8A.

The World Almanac and Book of Facts, New York, Newspaper Enterprise Association, 1985 and 1991 editions.

Yerkes, D., 'English language,' in *Academic American Encyclopedia*, electronic version, 1992.

Index